MAIN LIBRARY

STO

ACPL ITEM
DISCARDED

Y0-ABH-899

6-10-80

REDBOOK'S GUIDE TO BUYING YOUR FIRST HOME

EXPERT, EASY-TO-UNDERSTAND ADVICE AND PRACTICAL MONEY-SAVING IDEAS

•

Houses, Co-ops, Condominiums, Kit Houses, Renovations, Mobile Homes

•

Financing

•

Investments, tax shelters and inflation hedges

•

Rating a neighborhood

•

Judging a home's assets and flaws

•

PLUS checklists · worklists · questionnaires · interviews with home buyers, lenders and realtors · and much more

by Ruth Fairchild Pomeroy with the Editors of Redbook Magazine

FIRESIDE

*A Complete Guide
to the Decisions, the Selection,
the Financing, the Moving In,
and the Eventual Joys of
Establishing a First Home*

Redbook's Guide to

BUYING YOUR
FIRST HOME

By Ruth Fairchild Pomeroy

with the Editors of Redbook Magazine

64

A FIRESIDE BOOK · PUBLISHED BY
SIMON AND SCHUSTER · NEW YORK

80 2546 3

Copyright © 1980 by Redbook Publishing Company
All rights reserved
including the right of reproduction
in whole or in part in any form
A Fireside Book
Published by Simon and Schuster
A Division of Gulf & Western Corporation
Simon & Schuster Building
Rockefeller Center
1230 Avenue of the Americas
New York, New York 10020
FIRESIDE and colophon are trademarks of Simon & Schuster

Designed by Eve Kirch
Manufactured in the United States of America

1   2   3   4   5   6   7   8   9   10

Library of Congress Cataloging in Publication Data

Pomeroy, Ruth Fairchild, date.
    Redbook's guide to buying your first home.
    (A Fireside book)
    Bibliography: p.
    Includes index.
    1. House buying.   I. Redbook magazine.   II. Title.
III. Title: Guide to buying your first home.
HD1379.P65   643'.12   79-27492

ISBN 0-671-25385-9

Contents

Introduction

If the idea of buying a house is becoming an obsession with you, but you're terrified of making a mistake or tying up too much money—and wondering if you'll really like it once you get there—stop worrying. You are not alone.

To prepare this guide, the editors of *Redbook* magazine interviewed many first-home buyers whose experiences ran the gamut from spectacular success to disappointment and failure —with a surprising number managing to snatch victory from the jaws of defeat. We talked with people who made the jump with more courage than cash, with cautious investors, with people who found themselves in incredibly "lucky" circumstances, with people who'd made unwise decisions and had to get out of them.

Some, like Patricia and Gedney Howe, did a little research on themselves and the housing market before they began. With a very limited budget, they made careful decisions at the right time and, in a short period of time, have "traded up" to where, as Gedney puts it, "We're living in a castle."

In 1973, the Howes bought a 1,200-square-foot, two story house in the Ansonboro section of Charleston, South Carolina, for $22,000. The house was essentially four rooms, two up and two down. But each room had a fireplace, albeit somewhat covered over and not in wonderful shape. A previous owner had added a kitchen and back porch. At first glance, the house might have seemed undistinguished, even a mess to the untutored eye, but a mess of possibilities to the Howes. And it was in a good neighborhood.

By working nights and weekends (Patricia was going to law school and Gedney was getting started in his law business in Charleston), they "excavated" the fireplaces, built a deck out over the back porch and kitchen, put up a flat-topped tool shed in the backyard on which they planted a roof garden, and generally refurbished the house.

Approximately five years and uncountable hours of labor later, they sold the house for $70,000. They then bought one of the oldest houses in Charleston, known there as "the Calhoun Mansion." It, too, was in need of extensive restoration and repair. While that was going on, the Howes lived in one room with a hot plate, and Gedney claims to have lived on Granola bars for breakfast for four months.

Today, however, the old house is fully restored and a showplace. By day, while the Howes are at work, the house is shown commercially as a landmark, a great source of pride to the couple. After five each afternoon, it turns back into their dream house. And should their dreams change radically, the mansion is worth upwards of a small fortune.

Arlene Walsh had never thought much about buying a house at all. But when a new job took her from New York City to Los Angeles, she bought a house in the Hollywood Hills. "I guess it was because I expected it to be a good investment," she admits, "and everybody was into house buying."

She wasn't all wrong, as it turned out, but "I got into the house and hated it. I just hated it! I hated worrying about the lawn and I didn't want to go home at night."

She decided to get out, but it took a few hundred dollars worth of "instant decor"—some brightly colored floor seaters, plants (lots of plants), and some posters—to make the place look bright, young, attractive, and saleable. When Arlene hadn't sold before heavy rains drove some rodents down from the hills and into her basement, she faced a large extermination fee.

But she couldn't afford to abandon her initial investment, and she'd been right about one thing—a house, particularly one in an area like the Hollywood Hills, is a good investment. By sticking to her guns and doing whatever seemed reasonable to make the house marketable, she not only sold it, but made a profit. And at last report, she was looking to put her profits *not* into a rental but into a condominium, which, she confesses, "is what I should have done in the first place."

Some people we interviewed leaped a lot faster and looked even less than Arlene did into the whole process of buying a house. Bob and Carrie Westbrook (not their real names) were living in a one-bedroom apartment when their daughter was born, and decided a house was their next need. They went house hunting the following weekend, saw a house they liked, put a bid on it, and lost to a higher bidder. The next weekend, they saw a house they liked even better, bid for it, and lost again.

By the third weekend, they were so anxious, they signed an agreement to buy and put money down on a house they were pleased to think was "the best we'd seen yet."

Only after committing themselves did they ask Carrie's father, who was a builder, to visit their house with them. On cursory inspection, he found that the breezeway had once been a happy home to termites, the house was in a low-lying area that threatened to produce a chronic case of damp cellar, and the septic tank had problems. Today, the Westbrooks are wallowing in repair bills and misery.

"The American Dream" is the expression most frequently used to describe the pride of ownership, the symbol of accomplishment, the privacy and freedom of possessing your own home. But for first-time buyers, the whole project can seem so bewildering and filled with fear, it can look more like "The Impossible Dream." The financial investment is, after all, the largest you've probably made to date, which can make the emotional investment fraught with insecurity and indecision.

Redbook's Guide to Buying Your First Home is designed to replace that confusion with good, solid knowledge, and to allay your fears by letting you share the experiences of many who've already been there—the folks you've already heard from and the many others you'll be hearing from shortly. These are real people[1] who've already been through many of the frustrations and much of the decision making you'll face as a first-home buyer. And like generous missionaries, they are willing to share, advise, and even hold your hand over the pitfalls and through the pleasures. All agree that the search for a house should be a thrill, not a terror. All agree that there are definite ways to minimize, if not eliminate, the chances of making a really big mistake. And all agree that there is more than one reason for buying a house.

At one time, the primary urge to own a home was, for most people, motivated simply by the wish to have a place of their own where they could create a way of living that would make them happy. "To be free forever of apartment-house-beige walls and to build shelves where *I* want them," was the dream of one home buyer. But today, almost without exception, the people we talked with were also looking at a home as a good financial investment. While home values are bound to fluctuate with supply and demand, historically a home has proven to be a good long-term investment. One recent study[2] titled one of their graphs "No Place Like Home for Your Money." It showed that in the ten-year period from 1966 to 1976 the cash growth on a new, median-priced, conventionally financed, single-family house outperformed stocks, bonds, and savings accounts.

In addition to the investment angle, many young first-home buyers, especially singles and two-worker families without dependents, were seeking the immediate advantage of the tax shelter that comes with home ownership and about which you'll be reading lots as we go along.

---

1. Some real people asked that their names be changed to protect individuals they dealt with who were not so innocent.
2. *Study of Single Family Home Ownership,* conducted by American Standard, Inc.

In many instances, relief from rising rent costs was the big factor. But to a person, our home-buyers insisted that investment be top priority since it was the one factor that could get you out of a "mistake" without losing your shirt. It was certainly a help to Arlene Walsh when she decided it was a condominium and not a house she wanted. A large part of the Howes' investment was their own labor, but rising house and property costs in good areas helped them—and other first-home buyers —to trade up from houses they could afford to homes that fulfilled their dreams. It's the factor that might have released the Westbrooks from their bondage—and may do so yet as we read along. For even in terms of investment, one family's nightmare could turn out to be another family's dream.

All of the financial considerations of a home purchase take considerable juggling of the budget and weighing of figures to make an objective investment decision that's right for you. Unfortunately, the wish to also find a home you'll love to live in tends to be somewhat of an emotional decision and takes a completely different set of evaluations. When you couple the wish side of your search with the wariness needed to invest wisely, and add to those the fact that you're about to go into a market that's new to you, and begin to hear a language you've never heard before, about a product you've never owned before, it *can* be fearsome. But it can also all be straightened out.

To help you keep your priorities in order, you'll find each section in this book contains a checklist. They're there to be used so no question—about you, your housemates, your potential purchases—goes unasked or unanswered, and no important detail is overlooked or forgotten. And they'll save you all those spare pieces of paper you might be tempted to take notes on, and which inevitably get lost. You'll also find, at the end of the book, a Home Buyer's Dictionary to help you with the language of real estate.

But back to our real people, for a moment, those brave pioneers who we think are responsible for the basic backbone of this guide. Between them, they have gone into every type of housing imaginable—from small, fully furnished homes to big empty barns, from brand-new houses all the way back to genuine antiques, from condominiums and cooperatives to mobile homes and prefabs. A courageous few even built their own homes. Their experiences and decisions, the right ones and, perhaps more important, the ones they wish they hadn't made, have dictated the makeup of this guide. Its purpose is to help you look at all your options—and the consequences inherent in each—before, during, and after your search for a home and the money to buy it, and to help you make the best decisions for *you* all along the way. Happy hunting!

1

Taking Stock

Without exception, every experienced home buyer we interviewed said, "Think it all through and know what you really want." This chapter is designed to help you think through what you want, what you can afford, and what you need to provide a life-style that will please you. Admittedly, getting out and looking at homes you might buy sounds far more exciting than sitting at home and taking stock of your money, your possessions, and you. But if you do your stock taking thoughtfully and thoroughly, it will make a lot of later decisions much simpler and it will help you to avoid the most costly mistake of all: impulse buying. Simply by filling in the checklists in each of the three sections in this chapter, you'll learn a lot about how you choose to live, and whether you want to go for a dream house now or start more simply; you may even discover that what you thought you wanted isn't at all what you decide, once you've thought through your priorities.

TAKING STOCK OF YOUR MONEY

When you start to look at your options—the kind of home you want to buy—you'll find a wide variation in the amount of money you need to get into a home. (That's next, in Chapter 2.) Whether you end up being courageous and spending to the hilt of your buying power, or being cautious and spending only a portion of your savings, now is the time to add up all your available funds.

Savings.   It's easy enough to check your savings account balance, but you may have available assets (savings) in other forms that you want to consider applying to a home purchase. *Stocks and bonds* can be included as savings. List them at their current market value, but keep a check on them and remember that you'll have to deduct the cost of commission if you sell. *Savings certificates,* certificates of deposit, or money market certificates should only be considered as available funds if they have matured or will mature soon. It is likely you will lose the interest to be gained on such deposits if you withdraw them before the specified deposit time.

Life insurance loans.   If you have an insurance policy that has accumulated cash value, you can borrow up to that accumulated value from your insurance company at, usually, a very favorable interest rate.

Private loans and gifts.   A significant 12 percent of first-home buyers interviewed between April and June, 1977, received down-payment help in the form of gifts. Another 3 percent got a loan (usually from relatives), and 1½ percent reported using a combination.[1] In 1979, Michael Whatley, president of the American Building and Remodeling Company in Columbia, South Carolina, estimated it would be a "low ball-park figure" to say that one-third of the young couples buying old homes in that city were receiving help from their parents. When we asked Doyle Stuckey, of Doyle Stuckey Homes in Houston, Texas, how

1. *Home Ownership: Affording the Single Family Home,* prepared by the United States League of Savings Associations, Economics Department.

young people were managing to make the 20 percent down payments on $50,000 homes, he said, "Their parents help them. The parents see it as a good investment." If this route is available to you, talk it over with your relatives in a position to help. If it isn't, don't be discouraged. In the 1977 survey above, four out of five first-home buyers taking conventional loans from savings and loan associations used only savings to make their down payments.

Your regular income or incomes. This, too, is easy if all the wage earners are salaried employees. If not, it's best to average out the past two or three years' income, hoping, of course, that this will be a better year and permit some luxuries. Unless such extras as *bonus earnings* or *employee profit-sharing plans* are firmly predictable, either don't include them in your regular earnings or enter them at the lowest possible value.

Dividends and interest. Include interest or dividend returns only on those savings or investments that you *don't* plan to use toward the purchase of a home.

That's the income. Now, do you know where it's currently going? If you're a meticulous budgeter, this won't be difficult. If you've been more of a "mental" accountant, this is the time to get on paper your nonhousing expenses so the bottom line will be an indication of what you can spend per month on a house. The essentials like food, clothing, and medical care and the probables like insurance, commutation, recreation, and installment debts are listed in the checklist for this section. What's just as important now is to list expenses that are really important to you in terms of your short-term needs and your long-term goals. Both of those will likely be quite different for every individual person or family.

Looking At Immediate, Short-Term Money Needs

This is the place to take into account anything that's important to you that costs money. If, for example, a continuing education is a wanted, immediate goal and one you feel you shouldn't sacrifice, list it as a needed expense.

If you're in the process of starting a new business or planning to expand the one you have, forecast fairly the money that will take. Home buyers who have plowed everything into their new housing expenses have said, "You can really get to resent the place if you have to give up *everything* you want to do just to keep up payments."

Looking At Your Long-Term Money Needs

Whatever long-term goals are yours, they will affect your savings allowance now. That's why you'll find several blank spaces under savings in this section's checklist. Several first-home buyers we talked to said, "Savings? We just didn't have *any* for the first few years after we bought the house." The most-often voiced needs for savings were "We want to plan to have a family" and "We want to start now to be ready to pay for the children's education." Your long-term goal may be to have a vacation home, own your own business, or fly your own airplane. You're the only judge of your hopes and how important they are to work for. Maybe they can be postponed or maybe you'll feel better if you're setting aside even a small amount of investment toward them.

Now you should be ready to fill in Checklist 1a, Taking Stock of Your Money. Because it may take some time for you to find a home, there's a column to record any changes in income and needs that occur between now and the time you are ready to buy.

TAKING STOCK OF YOUR POSSESSIONS

If listing and measuring—yes, measuring—your possessions at this point seems premature, take Tom and Barbara Swenson's word that it isn't. Because there were multiple owners involved, they'd waited out long delays before getting into a lovely old house in Maplewood, New Jersey. It had natural chestnut woodwork throughout the house and, as Tom describes it, "crafts-

manship that would not be reproducible today." Finally came
moving day. All the carefully marked furniture and boxes were
being placed in their designated rooms except for the second-
floor bedroom furniture, which was sitting in the middle of the
living room—it was too big to go up the narrow stairway. Tom
wanted to dismiss the moving men. Barbara was in tears. Tom
figured that the movers were doing nothing but scratching their
heads at $40 an hour and he could scratch his for nothing. The
eventual solution to getting the furniture from the middle of the
living room to the bedroom entailed removing several stair
steps, piece by numbered piece, to make way for the move.
When, after three years in the house, Tom's job necessitated a
move to California, everyone groaned at the thought of taking
apart and putting back those much-admired, old chestnut stairs.

Most first-home buyers moving from an apartment to a house
will probably have to take all of their possessions with them to
fill the additional space of a house. But if your move is to a
condominium or a co-op apartment or a furnished manufactured
home, knowing what you want to take with you and how, where,
and if it will fit becomes crucial. Also, taking stock of your
possessions at this early stage helps you get a clear idea of
what's important to you; it can influence what you're really
looking for in a home.

Whether it's your Aunt Martha's corner cupboard or your
African violets or your art collection or the family cat that you
treasure, knowing what they are will help you visualize whether
they, too, will be at home in the place you contemplate buying.

Betty Christy, who recently moved into a new home in a
suburb of Washington, D.C., said she wouldn't have changed
her selection of her house had she realized, before she moved
in, that Timothy, a cocker spaniel, had never learned to go up
and down steps, now a necessity to get outdoors. Betty allowed
there would always be adjustments to make. "But," she said,
"it does make you feel pretty silly to crawl downstairs backwards on your hands and knees making barking noises to get a
baffled and frightened fourteen-year-old dog to follow you."

Remember your hobbies when you're taking stock of possessions. It's not too difficult to find space for a needlework frame, but an artist's studio needs a good light, and a woodworking shop has to have an area that will accommodate the equipment and can be shut off to avoid sending dust throughout the house.

Consider carefully whether you want to take along such furnishings as rugs, curtains, and draperies. Unless you have a beautiful oriental rug or have a fabric you love in draperies that you think can be cut to fit other windows or used to make pillows, you might be better off trying to sell them to the next tenant of your present home.

When you measure furniture and appliances, be sure to record height, depth, and width.

Checklist 1b, Taking Stock of Your Possessions, was meant to be flexible. Add to it as your possessions dictate. There's also space to indicate how important they are to you, an evaluation that will help you eliminate excess later, if necessary.

TAKING STOCK OF YOU

This is the real soul-searching inventory. And it is, without doubt, the hardest one to do. Most often, a move means that you'll be putting yourself in a new environment with new space to occupy, new neighbors to know or not to know, perhaps a new commute to work, and, depending upon the type of home you choose, a whole new set of responsibilities. It's not easy to project yourself into a place you've never been.

Now's a good time to start talking to people who have made a move—from city apartment to suburbia, from an old house to a new one, from a rented apartment to a cooperative apartment, from a country house to a city rehabilitation project. Find out what they've liked and what they haven't liked about their move and, meantime, keep analyzing your own preferences until you're fairly sure about what you want.

When Richard and Trisha Hobby went house hunting to get out of their cramped, drab, northern-exposure apartment on New York's Upper West Side, they liked the first house they

Checklist 1a. TAKING STOCK OF YOUR MONEY

Available Funds	Date Entered	Changes
Savings	$ _____	$ _____
Investments, such as stocks, bonds, mutual funds	_____	_____
Insurance loan (cash value)	_____	_____
Other available funds, such as: Personal loans	_____	_____
Gifts	_____	_____
Other	_____	_____
Total Available Funds (1)	$ _____	$ _____

Average Monthly Income	Date Entered	Changes
Take-home pay (gross pay less all deductions, such as taxes, pension, insurance) of all wage-earners who will participate in home purchase	$ _____	$ _____
Income from private business (less all taxes and deductions)	_____	_____
Dividends and interest (use only if investment will *not* be used for other available funds, above)	_____	_____
Bonuses, profit-sharing income	_____	_____
Other income	_____	_____
Total Average Monthly Income (A)	$ _____	$ _____

Average Monthly Nonhousing Expenses	Date Entered	Changes
Food, beverages, household supplies	$ _____	$ _____
Clothing	_____	_____

Checklist 1a. TAKING STOCK OF YOUR MONEY

Average Monthly Nonhousing Expenses	Date Entered	Changes
Personal care (barber, dry cleaning, hair dresser, etc.)	_____	_____
Medical and dental care (include medical insurance other than that deducted from wages)	_____	_____
Insurance (divide annual premiums by 12):	_____	_____
Life	_____	_____
Automobile	_____	_____
Personal property	_____	_____
Other	_____	_____
Automobile expenses and/ or commuting costs	_____	_____
Installment payments (include interest charges)	_____	_____
Recreation and hobbies	_____	_____
Education	_____	_____
Income tax beyond withholding	_____	_____
Contributions, dues, fees	_____	_____
Telephone	_____	_____
Regular savings (adjust to immediate and long-term needs)		
_____	_____	_____
_____	_____	_____
_____	_____	_____
Total Average Monthly Nonhousing Expenses (B)	$ _____	_____

Money Available for Monthly Housing Expenses	Date Entered	Changes
A. Total Average Monthly Income	$ _____	$ _____
B. Total Average Monthly Nonhousing Expenses	_____	_____
Deduct B from A for *Total Money Available for Monthly Housing Expenses* (C)	$ _____	$ _____

Checklist 1b. TAKING STOCK OF YOUR POSSESSIONS

Furniture	Measurement	Must Keep	Want to Keep, But
Bedroom(s)			
_____	_____	_____	_____
_____	_____	_____	_____
_____	_____	_____	_____
_____	_____	_____	_____
_____	_____	_____	_____
_____	_____	_____	_____
_____	_____	_____	_____
_____	_____	_____	_____
_____	_____	_____	_____
_____	_____	_____	_____
Living Room			
_____	_____	_____	_____
_____	_____	_____	_____

Checklist 1b. TAKING STOCK OF YOUR POSSESSIONS

Furniture	Measurement	Must Keep	Want to Keep, But

Living Room

_____	_____	_____	_____
_____	_____	_____	_____
_____	_____	_____	_____
_____	_____	_____	_____
_____	_____	_____	_____
_____	_____	_____	_____
_____	_____	_____	_____
_____	_____	_____	_____
_____	_____	_____	_____
_____	_____	_____	_____

Dining Room

_____	_____	_____	_____
_____	_____	_____	_____
_____	_____	_____	_____
_____	_____	_____	_____
_____	_____	_____	_____
_____	_____	_____	_____
_____	_____	_____	_____
_____	_____	_____	_____

Checklist 1b. TAKING STOCK OF YOUR POSSESSIONS

Furniture	Measurement	Must Keep	Want to Keep, But
Kitchen (furniture and appliances)			
_____	_____	_____	_____
_____	_____	_____	_____
_____	_____	_____	_____
_____	_____	_____	_____
_____	_____	_____	_____
_____	_____	_____	_____
_____	_____	_____	_____
_____	_____	_____	_____
_____	_____	_____	_____
_____	_____	_____	_____
Outdoor			
_____	_____	_____	_____
_____	_____	_____	_____
_____	_____	_____	_____
_____	_____	_____	_____
_____	_____	_____	_____
_____	_____	_____	_____
_____	_____	_____	_____
_____	_____	_____	_____

Checklist 1b. TAKING STOCK OF YOUR POSSESSIONS

Accessories	Measurements	Must Keep	Want to Keep
(Lamps, pictures, hanging wall cabinets, etc.)			
_____	_____	_____	_____
_____	_____	_____	_____
_____	_____	_____	_____
_____	_____	_____	_____
_____	_____	_____	_____
_____	_____	_____	_____
_____	_____	_____	_____
_____	_____	_____	_____
_____	_____	_____	_____

Furnishings (Rugs and draperies)	Measurements	Must Keep	Could Leave
_____	_____	_____	_____
_____	_____	_____	_____
_____	_____	_____	_____
_____	_____	_____	_____
_____	_____	_____	_____
_____	_____	_____	_____
_____	_____	_____	_____

Other Space-Taking Possessions (hobby equipment, house, office equipment)	Measurements	Must Take	Could Put Elsewhere

Other Possessions (plants, animals)	Special Needs for Them

saw the first day out. What appealed was the sunlight, the airy porch, the space, and the attic room with a skylight, a place Trisha, an artist, could use as a studio. "We knew the water pressure was low and the roof in mediocre shape and the wiring inadequate," Richard confessed, "but it was the feel of all that space that was great. Also it was a good solid house. It reminded me of the home where I was raised in Virginia."

As it turned out, the yen for sunshine and memory, a tricky value at best, moved the Hobbys to buy the house. But then came the "dreary commute," the fact that Trisha was going to school one night a week in the city and didn't get home until after midnight, and the gradual discovery that, as Richard put it, "We really were city people. We didn't fit in that community. I enjoy a limited amount of yard work and I mowed my lawn, but everyone else manicured theirs."

It took eight months to sell the house in Pleasantville, New York, but the Hobbys are now happily renovating a brownstone in the Park Slope area of Brooklyn, where they plan to rent out one floor and live on two, where their commute is fifteen minutes as opposed to an hour and forty-five minutes, and where they find, for them, a "great neighborhood spirit" and "the joy of getting back to the museums." Richard says, "I didn't make much profit on the house, but we learned a lot about ourselves —the hard way."

Here are some of the questions you should be asking yourself:

How much space do you need?   This will be dictated largely by the size of your family at present and the size you expect it to be. Consider how much space you'll need for guests. Overnight guests may fare fine on a sofa bed in the living room, but if you anticipate longer visits from relatives who live far away, a real extra bedroom will be a more comfortable arrangement for all concerned. How much entertaining does your life-style demand? Will it be formal or informal? Do you need space for someone to have the privacy of a home office or a room to do homework from school or an office? Do your hobbies require special space?

How much land do you want?   If a rolling lawn and a garden and a backyard barbecue are all part of your dream, are you sure you'll enjoy the work involved in caring for them? Or can you build enough into your monthly housing expenditures to hire the lawn mowed and save the rose planting for yourself? If the whole idea of lawn mowing and hedge trimming and weeding a garden are not your idea of fun, maybe a town house or a condominium should be the kind of home you consider.

What does your work demand?   If you're a two-wage-earner family, and most first-home buyers are, you may have to consider some compromises, especially in choosing a location that makes commuting to work relatively easy for both of you. If you go in different directions at different times, will you need more than one car? Will gas availability allow two cars? Does the distance—or distances—from work make fuel availability a problem? If you have irregular work hours, is public transportation regular and reliable at all hours or will driving be a necessity?

Does your business now, or will it in the near future, require entertaining in your home? Is it appropriate that the entertaining be informal or formal? Will your business ambitions influence your choice of a community or neighborhood? (Every community has its "status" areas.)

How stable is your work both as to job and location? If you were out of a job, would you look for a new one in the same vicinity? Is there a possibility that you can anticipate a job transfer to another location with your company?

How do you feel about your career? Do you want to be available for a better job no matter where it's located? If you want to leave room to be flexible to go wherever the job offer looks good, the resale value of the home you choose should be high on your priorities when you buy.

What do your leisure preferences indicate?   This is a good time to think about what you really enjoy doing with your leisure time. If your weekends have been devoted to skiing or hiking or boating, just getting away from it all, you can do that from anywhere. Tennis buffs and golfers and bowlers can probably find fellow enthusiasts in almost any community. But if your leisure preferences veer more to the spectator variety—concerts, theater, museums—you will want to weigh just how far you really want to get away from it all.

Will children influence your decision?   If you'll need daytime help or a day-care center for a preschool child, put that high on your priorities list. Working mothers report that nothing can be more nerve-wracking than feeling that your child isn't being properly cared for. For the same reason, investigate the quality of the schools in the community you choose, or check reliable transportation if your children will be living a distance from desirable schools.

How much privacy do you want?   Oddly enough, the tightest living complexes, such as cooperative apartments or town houses, seem to breed the greatest degree of privacy. Condominiums provide about the same amount of privacy, depending upon how much use you make of the common recreational facilities. A house with no near neighbors may mean real privacy, but how will you feel about being that far away from other people? When Lou and Susan Lerner moved from a town house in Arlington, Virginia, where "the neighbors were completely unfriendly," into a manufactured (mobile) home park in Chantilly, Virginia, they loved the change. Lou said, "We have the freedom of our own house but the neighbors are nicer and we've made a lot of good friends out here." If you choose a small community as home, do you want to get involved in the life of the community? Does being a cup-of-sugar borrower or a drop-in-for-coffee neighbor appeal to you? If not, you might be considered unfriendly and end up feeling you don't fit.

Are you a person who really likes to putter around the house?   When a faucet develops a drip, do you get out the wrench and the washers and cure the problem, or have you always called in a superintendent or notified the landlord or, heaven forbid, tried to get a plumber to take care of such a minor annoyance? Have you found paper hanging a challenge, painting a room satisfying, caulking a bathtub a snap? If you're not only capable, but really enjoy working on the continual upkeep jobs a house entails, you'll love having a house of your own. If you aren't a natural-born putterer, figure on the cost of buying those assorted services or look for minimum upkeep when you choose your home.

What's your style? This may be the one emotional decision you have the luxury of making when you choose a home. A new ranch-style may be your dream, an Italianate town house may have aesthetics that appeal to you, a turn-of-the-century house with a porch, a split-level house with a patio, a sleek glass modern or a comfortable colonial or a log house may be what you have your heart set on. When Roz and Douglas Barden started house hunting, they were firm about wanting a Dutch colonial and (high priority) space for a garden. "We finally decided on a Cape Cod; it had that certain charm we wanted." When Ruth and Bill Robbins' old home on Shelter Island, New York, burned down, their son Scotty asked, "Daddy, can we build a new 'old' house?" Style is an individual taste and, happily, whether you're looking for a single-family house or a part of a multiple dwelling, there's likely to be something out there that appeals to everyone. Charm, like beauty, is in the eye of the beholder.

The checklist in this section, 1c, is for recording your own and your family's needs, priorities, and tastes.

Checklist 1c. TAKING STOCK OF YOU

How Much Space Do You Need/ Want?	Top Priority	Would Be Nice, but Not Necessary	Not Important
Four or more bedrooms	_____	_____	_____
Three bedrooms	_____	_____	_____
Two bedrooms	_____	_____	_____
A separate dining room	_____	_____	_____
An eat-in kitchen	_____	_____	_____
A good-sized living room	_____	_____	_____
A family room	_____	_____	_____
A home office	_____	_____	_____
A patio	_____	_____	_____
A garage: One-car	_____	_____	_____
Two-car	_____	_____	_____
Other _____	_____	_____	_____
_____	_____	_____	_____

How Much Land Do You Want?

	Top Priority	Would Be Nice, but Not Necessary	Not Important
At least one acre	_____	_____	_____
A front lawn	_____	_____	_____
Room for a garden	_____	_____	_____
Minimum lawn	_____	_____	_____
Other _____	_____	_____	_____
_____	_____	_____	_____

What Does Your Work Demand?	Top Priority	Would Be Nice, but Not Necessary	Not Important
Good public transportation at regular morning and evening hours	_____	_____	_____
At irregular hours	_____	_____	_____
An automobile for business	_____	_____	_____
Two automobiles	_____	_____	_____
Prospect of quick resale of home	_____	_____	_____
Room for informal business entertaining	_____	_____	_____
Room for formal business entertaining	_____	_____	_____
A "status" community	_____	_____	_____

What Do Your Leisure Preferences Indicate?

	Top Priority	Would Be Nice, but Not Necessary	Not Important
A place for an active sport or sports	_____	_____	_____
(list) _____	_____	_____	_____
_____	_____	_____	_____
_____	_____	_____	_____
_____	_____	_____	_____
_____	_____	_____	_____
Accessibility to: Continuing education	_____	_____	_____
Concerts	_____	_____	_____
Museums	_____	_____	_____
Theater	_____	_____	_____

Checklist 1c. TAKING STOCK OF YOU

What Do Your Leisure Preferences Indicate?	Top Priority	Would Be Nice, but Not Necessary	Not Important
Other _____	_____	_____	_____
_____	_____	_____	_____
_____	_____	_____	_____
Seeing friends often	_____	_____	_____
Other _____	_____	_____	_____
_____	_____	_____	_____
_____	_____	_____	_____

Will Children Influence Your Decision?			
Good day care for preschool child	_____	_____	_____
Good schools	_____	_____	_____
Reliable transportation to schools	_____	_____	_____
Extra activities available for children (such as music classes, swim club)			
_____	_____	_____	_____
_____	_____	_____	_____
_____	_____	_____	_____
Other _____	_____	_____	_____
_____	_____	_____	_____
_____	_____	_____	_____

How Much Privacy Do You Want?	Top Priority	Would Be Nice, but Not Necessary	Not Important
An impersonal apartment or condominium complex	_____	_____	_____
A house with great privacy	_____	_____	_____
A house with neighbors but not too close	_____	_____	_____
A house in a small family town or community	_____	_____	_____
A house in a development with close neighbors	_____	_____	_____
Other: _____	_____	_____	_____
_____	_____	_____	_____

What's Your Style?	Most Wanted	Second Choice	Third Choice	Doesn't Matter
Unless you have some firm opinions, you may want to come back to this after you've read Chapter 2, "What Are Your Options?"				
Old house	_____	_____	_____	_____
New house	_____	_____	_____	_____
Big house	_____	_____	_____	_____
Compact house	_____	_____	_____	_____

Checklist 1c. TAKING STOCK OF YOU

What's Your Style?	Most Wanted	Second Choice	Third Choice	Doesn't Matter
Two-family house	_____	_____	_____	_____
Apartment	_____	_____	_____	_____
Condominium	_____	_____	_____	_____
Town house	_____	_____	_____	_____
One-story house	_____	_____	_____	_____
One-and-a-half story house	_____	_____	_____	_____
Two- or three-story house	_____	_____	_____	_____
Style of house	_____	_____	_____	_____
_____	_____	_____	_____	_____
_____	_____	_____	_____	_____
_____	_____	_____	_____	_____

2

What Are Your Options?

2113512

HOW MUCH MONEY CAN YOU OR DO YOU WANT TO SPEND?

The traditional rules-of-thumb in the housing market say that a person or a family should not spend more than two to two-and-a-half times their annual household income on a home, and that the monthly housing expenses (including mortgage payments, interest, taxes, home insurance, fuel, utilities, maintenance, and repair) should not exceed 25 percent of the monthly income. Translated, this means that if your annual family income is $20,000, you should not entertain the idea of purchasing a home for more than $50,000 and should not contract to pay out more than $416.66 a month for all housing expenses.

There's one other rule in the home-buying market known as the 33⅓ percent rule, which may pertain to first-home buyers who may have other long-term installment debts, such as auto-loan payments. This says that total annual housing expenses, *plus* the total annual installment payments, should not exceed 33⅓ percent of your annual income. These rules are considered reasonable guidelines and are not always adhered to as fixed limitations by borrowers or lenders. There is also a way to combine the 25 percent and the 33⅓ percent rules. If you have no installment debts and don't intend to incur any immediately, you can expect to be able to meet higher monthly housing costs by substituting them for other debts.

In the 1977 survey of first-home buyers,[1] two-fifths of first-home buyers exceeded the 25 percent rule and 30 percent exceeded the 33⅓ percent rule.

A majority of first-home buyers were able to allocate a larger portion of their income to housing because they were young (63 percent were less than thirty), they had small households (66 percent were either one- or two-member households), and many were able to rely on two incomes. Their family responsibilities, such as education for children, were still years in the future and the wage earners could look to increasing earnings while their basic housing debt would remain stable even though taxes, fuel, and utilities might be expected to rise. If your responsibilities are greater than average, you may want to keep your monthly housing debt under 25 percent of your income. Whichever way you choose to use the rules, they are fair guidelines to start with.

However, lenders—the people to whom you'll apply for a mortgage—are aware of these rules-of-thumb and they too will use them along with other evaluations to judge your home-buying ability. But, and it's a big but, for many first-home buyers, those rules were designed to be useful as they applied to a standard fixed-payment mortgage, on which the monthly payments remain the same for the life of the mortgage. There is an alternate kind of mortgage which is especially appealing to young buyers who have confidence that their incomes will increase with their age and their job experience.

In the mortgage trade, this plan is called a graduated-payment mortgage (GPM), and it allows a buyer to make lower monthly payments during the early years of the loan, with payments increasing year by year until they reach a fixed level, five to ten

---

1. *Home Ownership*, U.S. League of Savings Associations.

years into the life of the loan. While these plans don't preclude the use of the 25 percent and 33⅓ percent rules, they do allow many people to buy a home they might not otherwise afford. These plans, once available only on FHA-insured mortgages and some state lending institutions, are now available nationally through federally chartered savings and loan institutions. More details on graduated mortgage financing will be found in Chapter 4. For the time being, you really want to get down to what you can afford for a down payment and what you want to spend, or can spend, on monthly housing.

How Much Down Payment Can You Afford?

A down payment is a percentage of the cost of a home which you are expected to pay at the time of purchase. It can vary from nothing, with a Veterans Administration Guaranteed Home Loan (often referred to as a GI or VA mortgage), to 3 percent to 5 percent with a Federal Housing Administration (FHA) insured loan and upward to 25 percent, depending upon the location and price of the home.

If determining how much you can spend for a down payment were as simple as finding your Total Available Funds—(1) from Checklist 1a—it would be easy but not realistic. You really have to come at a reasonable down payment figure backwards. And, at this point, you'll be better off to get a price range rather than an exact figure. You can't know now whether the home you plan to buy will come equipped with any necessary appliances such as a range or refrigerator, or any furnishings that might tide you over until you can invest in your own possessions.

There are unavoidable costs that will require cash when you buy, and you'll need to subtract those from your available funds to see what's left for the down payment.

Closing costs are not the least of these, and they can vary greatly depending upon where you choose to buy. The majority of these costs are fees and charges for such services as a title search, a property survey, a credit report on you, an appraisal fee, title insurance premium, an attorney's fee (the lender's attorney), notary fees, recording fees, and a mortgage origination fee. By law, a lender—(the person who gives you the mortgage money)— must give you a "good faith" estimate of these costs when you apply for a mortgage, but that will be a little late to help you figure your down-payment shopping power. Because these costs vary so greatly, from a few hundred dollars to a few thousand, or 1 percent to 8 percent of the cost of the house, you can use 4 percent of the house price to estimate what you'll need for closing costs. They have one happy aspect: they're one-time costs.

Though not technically closing costs, there are a number of other up-front expenses you may be asked to pay. One is *your portion of any fees or services* that have been paid in advance by the previous owner, such as real estate taxes, oil left in the heating-fuel tank, or a garbage collection service fee. You may need an advance deposit for the local utility company, and there will be installation charges for a telephone.

You will be required by the lender to carry *hazard insurance*. If you take out your own policy, you will have to show evidence of a premium payment, often an annual premium. However, you may find that your lender requires that each monthly payment include some money to go into an escrow account which will be used by the lender to pay insurance premiums and real estate taxes when they come due. If so, you may be asked to put down one-twelfth of that amount when you buy.

Other than these costs that may seem by now to be thrust upon you, there are costs you may choose or need to incur:

You may wish to have *your own lawyer*. Even though you're paying a lawyer's fee in your closing costs, that lawyer is acting in the best interests of the seller and the lender. Because of the enormous amount of paperwork involved in purchasing a home and getting a loan, most experienced buyers say you should have a lawyer, preferably one experienced in real estate. As much as anything else, he will be an interpreter for the legalese in which agreements are written, but he will also represent your interests in the transaction and be there to help you if the seller does not meet his obligations. A legal fee on a routine purchase should run between $150 and $200, although some lawyers ask 1 percent of the purchase price of the house. Be sure to have the fee settled when you engage the lawyer.

An appraiser or a *building inspector* will evaluate a home you plan to buy after you apply for a loan. He will be doing it for the interest of the lender and his report is available to you. Building inspection is a mandatory part of the mortgage agreement when you apply for a VA or an FHA mortgage loan. You may be satisfied to go with those evaluations, but if you're looking at an older house you may want to have a building inspector evaluate its condition and give you an estimate on the cost of needed repairs. His report should cost around $100 and it might give you much more bargaining power over the price of the home. *Necessary alterations or repairs* recognized through a building inspection may not have to be done immediately. If they can be postponed until you catch your financial breath, they won't have to be deducted from your down-payment estimation, but you should up your monthly maintenance and repair costs accordingly.

Furniture or furnishings may have to be part of your original cost of home ownership. Whether you plan to buy these out of available funds or purchase them on an installment plan, figure their purchase price either on your down payment calculation or on your monthly housing expenditure.

You might at this stage think of setting some money aside for either necessary repairs or furniture and furnishings. Buyers of old homes are more likely to make do with the furniture they have and use the extra money for repairs. Fran and Robert Mitilieri moved into a seventy-year-old, eleven-room house in Staten Island, New York, "with just our apartment furniture and some 'antiques' we'd picked up because we knew we had to replace the wiring immediately. When we moved in, we had to unplug the refrigerator before we used the toaster in the morning."

A move to a new house is more likely to necessitate at least new furnishings, some landscaping, and perhaps additional furniture. New-home buyers we talked to felt the urge "to have things look fixed up and finished as soon as possible." If, on the other hand, you're thinking of a cooperative apartment, a condominium, or a completely furnished, manufactured house (you might once have thought of these as mobile homes), you can ignore these costs for now.

Moving costs, whether you hire a truck and do it yourself or engage a moving firm to come in and do it all, are due the day of delivery. Build them into your budget.

And then there are *emergencies.* When Donna and Norman Johnson moved into their home in Stamford, Connecticut, they found they had no water; the well pump was broken and needed $400 worth of repair. When that was fixed and they moved in for the second time, they had water but none of it was hot. The hot-water heating unit was also broken and required a $300 repair. One interviewee who asked to be nameless was shocked by a $300 cockroach-extermination fee before she could move into her home in Georgetown, a fashionable section of Washington, D.C. It's best to keep an emergency fund. If it isn't needed, you might be able to afford that new sofa sooner than you thought.

How Much Monthly Maintenance Can You Afford?

You've already arrived at your Money Available for Monthly Housing Expenses (C in Checklist 1a). Out of that, your monthly *mortgage and interest payment* will undoubtedly be the biggest expense, but it is a set amount. *Property taxes* and *utility charges* are two costs that have been, and may continue to be, rising sharply. Unless you're very familiar with the general area in which you plan to buy, it's almost impossible to figure how much you'll need for these expenses now. As you start to look around, keep these two costs high on your list of questions. Ask not just what they are, but how fast they have been going up over the last five years.

Comprehensive insurance will be necessary. It may be included in your mortgage payments. If not, you will need a separate policy.

Maintenance and repair are an inherent part of home ownership. Experts say you should count on spending a minimum 1 percent of the price of your home each year. For an older home that needs some major repairs, you may have to allocate more for the first few years you're there. In a cooperative apartment or condominium, you may get by with less, especially if it is a relatively new building complex.

Installment payments on furniture or furnishings or major appliances, if you choose to buy them on a monthly payment plan, will need to be recorded here. So will installment payments on a second automobile if that's necessary with the move. While a lender will look at these as monthly expenses under the $33\frac{1}{3}$ percent rule, if they are new expenses not listed in Chapter 1, figure them as new monthly deductions.

Adding It All Up or Subtracting It All Down

Checklist 2a is not meant to be discouraging. It was designed to help you start your home hunting with some idea of what you can afford, and prevent you from unintentionally getting in over your head. We talked with a lot of people who bought a place to live almost totally with borrowed money, and were willing to give up a great many luxuries to have a home of their own. If that's your eventual decision, you can at least make it knowing what you're doing and avoiding what one observer, Walter Sosnowski, calls "the One Big Mistake: not leaving enough money after the closing to take care of the mortgage payment, the telephone, the gas and electric—all due on the first of the month."

Can You Afford the Monthly Housing Expense?

Unless you know the area in which you intend to buy or until you look at specific houses, there is no realistic way to guess at the monthly housing expenses. Now you are armed with your Money Available for Monthly Housing Expenses (C from Checklist 1a) and an idea of the costs over and above the mortgage payments. The next Checklist, 2b, appears here to remind

Checklist 2a. PRICE RANGE OF HOUSE WE CAN AFFORD

(2½ times your total annual income) $ _____ to $ _____

How Much Down Payment Can You Afford?

Total Available Funds—(1) from Checklist
   1a $ _____

Expected Cash Needs
   Closing costs (use 4 percent of median
              house cost) $ _____

Furniture and furnishings or
Expected alterations and repair
   (list here only if you don't plan to put
   these on a monthly payment schedule) $ _____

Real estate lawyer $ _____

Building inspector $ _____

Moving expenses $ _____

Emergency fund $ _____

Total Expected Cash Needs (2) $ _____

Subtract 2 from 1 to get
Amount You Can Afford for a Down
Payment (3) $ _____

you to ask the necessary cost questions when you find a specific home. Because you may have to use it more than once in calculating whether you can meet the monthly payments on the homes you look at and like, it is set up in a form that will allow you to use it for several evaluations.

SORTING OUT YOUR REASONS FOR BUYING

You've already thought through your short-term and long-term goals, which should have helped you make some decisions about what's important to you and where and how you'd like to live. Analyzing your motives for buying a home can also give you some other values to think about. "Having a place of our own" (that American Dream) was the reason we heard most often. But "getting out from under that high rent" or "not throwing away all that money on rent" were close seconds. Frequently, people were looking for a combination of reasons. Their decisions and why they made them may suggest some considerations you'll want to add to your own list of priorities.

The Long-Range, This-Is-It Reason

When the Militieris went house hunting in Staten Island, New York, in 1976, Fran and Bob were both working and had decided they wanted a house big enough for their future needs. "We overbought," Fran said of their two-family house, "but it was just what we wanted. We were looking for a big house so my Mom could have her private quarters and a place to live for the rest of her life. Eventually, we plan to populate it with a family of our own. Meanwhile, we'll keep improving the house. It all needs new insulation. Gradually, we'll fix it up the way we want it."

To reiterate the first-time costs of buying a house, Fran and Bob made a down payment of $9,400 on their $48,000 house, which they figured was worth from $55,000 to $60,000 in 1978.

"But," Fran remembered, "it cost us around $12,000 to settle, with closing costs and all."

Tom and Becky Hermann were married in June of 1978, a peak year for demand of houses and, as a result, high housing prices. Becky was selling Mopeds and Tom was working as a carpenter for Shandon Properties in Columbia, South Carolina. Their first housing was a two-bedroom rental, but they immediately started house hunting because, in Becky's words, "It's really stupid to rent a house in this U.S. economy." When they looked around in the $25,000–$30,000 price range they felt they could afford, they were shocked to find "we were looking at boxes."

After several months of looking and debating, they chose the long-range option and on December first of the year they married, and moved into an old, columned, two-story home in the Elmwood Park area of the city, two blocks from the Governor's Mansion. They were able to get a mortgage from the owner and paid around $20,000 for the eleven-room house.

When we talked with Tom and Becky, they were living upstairs, had ripped out all the paneling downstairs, and planned to refinish the painted floors. Their long-range plan: "To rent out the upstairs until we get our furniture and want children, then turn the upstairs kitchen into a master bathroom." They love the space—the foyer area is fifteen by fifteen feet, there are porches on both floors, their front windows are six by four feet, and their mortgage payments are cheaper than their former two-bedroom rental.

There are distinct advantages and disadvantages to the long-range decision, as there are to all the reasons for buying. One advantage is that your sights are set and everything you put into the house can be chosen to suit your tastes and needs and your way of life. But it also means that you must be certain you are happy with the style of the house, its location, and the neighborhood.

Also, you should be fairly certain that you want to stay to work and live where you buy. The long-range reason is not for you if you want the freedom to move wherever and whenever

Checklist 2b. CAN YOU AFFORD THE MONTHLY HOUSING EXPENSE?

Money Available for Monthly Housing Expense from Checklist 1a
Average monthly housing expense of (insert description of home at top of column)

Mortgage payment (principal and interest)

Comprehensive insurance (if not included in mortgage payment or if not bought separately at an annual premium)

Property taxes (if not included in mortgage payment)

Utilities (fuel for heating, gas/electric, water)

Maintenance and repairs

New installment payments, if any

Any other new monthly expenses

Total (D)

Compare D with C to check affordability of home in monthly expenses.

an opportunity may arise, or if you're not ready to invest a great deal of your own effort and money in a home now. Both the Hermanns and the Militieris bought space to spare for the future. If you're looking at an idyllic small house as a long-range investment, with the thought of adding to it, you will have to be sure the land that comes with your house provides enough space for expansion. Also check your frontage and local zoning laws, which may dictate how close you can build to the street or to your next-door neighbor.

The disadvantage of the long-term reason for buying, especially for first-home purchasers, is that tastes and needs often change. If you feel confident that you know what you want, go ahead. If you have doubts, give it more thought or back your decision up with other reasons to buy.

The Not-Throwing-All-That-Money-Away-on-Rent Reason

Lou and Susan Lerner were not married when they began to feel they were burdened by the $425 monthly rent they were paying for a town house in Arlington, Virginia. Lou said, "We just found we had to cut down on things we liked to do, and I resented the idea that someone else was making all that money. One Sunday, we decided to drive around and see what we could find. We went into this place that looked like a subdivision, nice wide streets and curbed sidewalks. It turned out to be a mobile park in Chantilly, Virginia, about four miles from Dulles Airport." In this park you own your home and rent the land. Lou and Susan bought an $11,000 home there with a $1,000 down payment, and now pay $251 a month for their housing ($140 on the mortgage that Sue got through her credit union and $111 for the lot rental). When we asked if they had been concerned about co-ownership of a house as a "single couple," Lou allowed they had not. But since they are married now, all is legally fine anyway.

Donna Holt, a single woman in Houston, Texas, getting a rent increase every six months, bought a new, $49,000, three-bedroom home on which she had to put $10,000 down, and has monthly housing costs of about $500. While that's more money per month than she was paying for rent, she figures she's got a good house with a high resale value and is really ahead of the game, because "friends who live in the apartment house I was in are now paying $800 and $900 a month for one-bedroom units. Also, my monthly payments are fixed while rents will probably be increasing." You'll be hearing lots more about cold-cash advantages for home owners as we go along.

In 1974, Teri Thomas was working in a New York hospital. She picked up an employee's newsletter to read over lunch and spotted an ad for a three-and-a-half room cooperative apartment selling for $15,000, with a maintenance charge of $118 a month. (Both the initial cost and the maintenance were very low for that size apartment in a good location in New York City.) "All afternoon I kept wondering what an apartment facing Central Park could be like for $118 a month," Teri told us. "Anyway, I decided to go take a look out of sheer curiosity. I got there, loved the trees on the street, went in, and found it was really a four-and-a-half-room: They hadn't counted the dining room. Suddenly I found myself saying, in a very ladylike voice, 'I'm very interested in this apartment. Please don't show it to anyone else for a week. I'll speak to my lawyer.' When I came out of my daze I realized I needed a $3,000 down payment and I had closer to $300 in the bank. Also, I had no lawyer. I never would have gone back, except that I told a friend of mine who knew a lot about apartment values, and she persuaded me that we should go back together and look at it. That time I saw only the doctor's-green walls and an army of cockroaches, but my friend saw a real bargain."

With financial help from family and friends, Teri bought the apartment—and wouldn't sell it at twice the price she paid, which she's been offered.

Making the financial decision to buy rather than to rent must be an individual judgment. It will depend to a large extent upon what is available to buy in your area (see "Have You Checked Out All the Possibilities?" later in this chapter.) As a general rule, over the long haul it will pay to buy. For example, let's say you make a 20 percent down payment. That means 80 percent of the money for your house is being put up by the lender. You'll pay the lender back month by month with, in time of inflation, dollars that are less valuable than the ones he put up for you. Each month, you're owning a little more of your home which should be increasing in value, and that value belongs to you, not the lender. Every month your share of the home ownership (your equity) increases and that's more akin to putting money into a savings account than giving it to a landlord. Also, once you've owned a home for two or three years and your home ownership share (equity) has increased, you should reach a break-even point where your up-front payments have been absorbed and your monthly housing cost is equal to or less than the rental of a similar house or apartment. The longer you own a house, the cheaper it is compared to renting a similar house or apartment. And we haven't even gotten to all the cash values and advantages outside of equity.

In the first few years, it may cost you more to buy, as it did Donna Holt. That is most typical because of the up-front costs of purchasing a home. But with a traditional fixed-rate mortgage or buyer's mortgage, payments will remain the same over the twenty to thirty-year life of the mortgage, while renters' costs probably will be going up.

There is another financial advantage for home buyers, especially for single people and couples with no dependents. It is the "tax shelter" provided through the federal tax laws that allows deductions to home owners that are not available to renters. That is a major reason that motivates many first-home buyers to purchase. Mortgage interest, state and local real estate and property taxes, some moving, maintenance, and repair expenses in the year they are paid, "points" charged by banks for mortgages in the year they are paid—are all allowable deductions.

The Tax Shelter Reason

Sandy and David Spaeth both had good jobs and they had no dependents—in short, they paid lots of income tax on their salaries and had no deductions. They went house hunting for the specific reason of acquiring a tax break. In 1973, they found a 165-year-old, two-story home in the old whaling village of Sag Harbor, New York. It needed a new roof, new plumbing, and new wiring, but it was the first home in town that had been built with central heating, and some furniture came with the house which Sandy described as one-half nice pieces and one-half awful. They've been working on the house and the grounds—the crab grass was their nemesis—and eventually will rent out the second floor apartment, "but only to friends." Meanwhile, they get lots of deductions for all that really necessary repair work, are building up their equity while the value of their property rises—and they can still look forward to a small rental income before they're through.

To figure how home ownership would provide a tax shelter for you, you'll need to know what tax bracket you're in, what portion of your expected monthly payments will be for interest on the loan, and approximately what your real estate taxes will be. If you're not a mathematical whiz, this would be a good time to get out your pocket calculator—or acquire one. It will come in handy when you begin the search for your home and your money to buy it.

This is a just-suppose example of the way *mortgage interest* and *real estate taxes* would affect your federal income tax:

If you bought a $40,000 home with 10 percent down payment and took a $36,000 loan (mortgage) at 9 percent (your interest rate) for 30 years, your monthly payment on the mortgage would be $289.67. The payment averages out during the first year to $37.67 paid on the principal of the loan. The interest averages to $252.00 per month. With each month's payment, you're paying a little more toward the principal and a little less for interest, but in the early years of a mortgage, the interest might be larger than you'd expect. And it is tax deductible. If your property taxes are $100 per month, this makes a total monthly outlay of $389.67. Of that amount, the interest of $252.00 and the property taxes of $100.00 are tax deductible for a total of $352.00 per month, or $4,224.00 ($352.00 × 12) per year. (All you need is an interest statement from your mortgage holder and a property tax statement from your township or county.)

If you are in the 25 percent tax bracket, your annual tax saving, on the foregoing figures, would be $1,056.00 ($4,224.00 × .25) or $88.00 ($1,056.00 ÷ 12) per month. In effect, that would reduce your monthly housing cost to $301.67 ($389.67 − $88.00) per month. In addition, you may find that you can deduct costs of maintenance and repair in the year these are paid.

In general, all home owners can benefit from tax deductions, but the actual savings will obviously be greater to those in higher tax brackets. For example, if all other figures in the example above were the same and your tax bracket were 35 percent, your annual saving would be $1,478.40 ($4,224.00 × .35), or $123.20 ($1,478.40 ÷ 12) per month. As you can see, compared with the figures in the 25 percent bracket, savings can rise rapidly with your income.

The Good Investment Reason

Making a good investment really ought to be high priority for any home buyer, but it probably should be primary to all first-home buyers who are often looking ahead to moving on to a bigger and better house as their incomes and families increase. If making a good investment is your motivation for buying, you may have to sacrifice some of your personal likes and dislikes, or at least take them off the top of the list. A tiny "doll house," for example, might be appealing to you if you are single and looking for something not too much bigger than the apartment you plan to leave. But the odds on the number of people who will be looking for a doll house are not great. You may have a long wait to find someone who wants to buy it.

The same may be true of an overly large house, unless it has been renovated or can be renovated to make portions of it rentable. The soaring cost of heating fuel alone may make a big house a white elephant. A house that has a highway scheduled to be built close to it is certainly not a good investment. But these are questions you'll ask when you begin your search. Realtors know what constitutes the most desirable homes for resale, and if that's what you're looking for, it should be part of the information you give the person who's helping you locate a house.

We found two distinct kinds of Good Investment buyers: One group said their primary purpose was to "build equity," and the other group was building "leverage." Because there are different implications to each of these investment terms, it's a good idea to understand what each of them means before you start your search for either money or a house. You'll probably hear the terms whenever you talk to home-owning friends or investors.

Equity is simply the difference between the value of your home and what you owe on the mortgage. With each payment you make on your home, you are reducing your mortgage and consequently increasing your equity. But if your home is increasing in value, you're also increasing your equity. It's not unlike thinking of your mortgage payments as enforced savings and the appreciation of your home as interest on those savings. Equity is an asset on your personal financial statement. If you ever need to cash in on it, it's there like a savings account.

Suppose you bought a $40,000 house and put 20 percent down to get a $32,000 mortgage. In five years, your house increases in value to $50,000. (You can have a house appraised for value.) You could then refinance your home with a $40,000 mortgage (still with 20 percent down), pay off the $32,000 mortgage, and have an $8,000 difference, less any refinancing charges. You might have needed to use your equity for an emergency or a school tuition.

If you had chosen to take the $8,000 and reinvest it, that would be *leveraging*. You'd be using money to make money—a more sophisticated game that you shouldn't take on unless you feel capable of playing, or have the ability to pay for some good advice.

The Buying-to-Sell Reason

Karen and Ralph Connit, both working in San Francisco, having no dependents, looked at the tax shelter of home ownership, but they also went into the market with a plan to resell. A good neighborhood and a sound house were their priorities. In February, 1975, they found an eleven-year-old home located "right on the edge of trendy Hillsborough." Karen told us, "The location was right, the house was rather underpriced and physically perfect, but anyone looking for a home to love might have overlooked it. It had pea-green walls in the old-fashioned kitchen, gaudy wallpaper, and 1950s pink-and-gray tiles in the bathrooms." The owner was willing to let them have a thirty-year mortgage at 10 percent down on the $64,000 house. Karen and Ralph spent about two and a half years of work and $20,000 of their own money (half of which went for a modern kitchen) before they sold the house for $136,000 in July, 1977.

The Increase-in-Value Reason

When the Shaw neighborhood in Washington, D.C., was undergoing intensive rehabilitation in 1978, George and Michele Martin opted to buy an old home just a few blocks ahead of the rehabilitation activity. They put 10 percent down for their $65,000, 1909 house, yard, garage, and alley. They figure they've got a good investment for a house with a full basement, two living floors, and an attic they will eventually rent out. Currently, they have a friend who's a carpenter living in it rent-free in exchange for some valuable help in the refurbishing.

Both the Connits and the Martins were gambling some—the Connits with their belief that they could make their reasonably well-placed house attractive enough for a high resale price, the Martins with the belief that the upward trend of the Shaw neighborhood will catch up with them and increase the value of their property and ultimate equity.

Buying as an investment will always have some element of risk, but buying housing—if you choose well—still has the best record on the market.

To sort out your own reasons for buying, use Checklist 2c.

Checklist 2c. MY PRIORITIES FOR BUYING

Use Column 1 as top priority, Column 2 as important, and Column 3 as unimportant or doesn't matter.

	1	2	3
A home we will like for a long time			
A home that will reduce our monthly housing cost			
A home that has good resale value			
Ownership for tax shelter purposes			
Getting something we own, to build equity			
A sound house we can improve to sell			
A house that offers space for a rental portion			

HAVE YOU CHECKED OUT ALL THE HOUSING POSSIBILITIES?

When people think about buying a home they most often think "house," and while it's true that the detached, single-family house has been the most sought-after home, a great variety of styles and sizes and prices exist among those alone. But the tremendous growth has been in multifamily housing that offers the opportunity of ownership. Condominiums, cooperative apartments, town houses, and cluster houses have proliferated in the late 1970s, and they can offer a route to home ownership that may be a good interim step from apartment rental to house. There are also schools that teach people how to build houses, and a great many first-home owners have substituted "sweat equity" for dollars to achieve a home they could afford. And then there are houseboats—yes, houseboats. A recent count in the waters around Seattle reported more than 600 houseboats serving as primary homes, and ranging in value from a few thousand dollars to a quarter of a million.

There are old houses and new houses, houses that are available for renovation and restoration, manufactured houses that come in panels ready to be erected on your land, precut manufactured houses that many people opt to build themselves from packaged instructions, completely furnished manufactured homes (once known as mobile homes) that are delivered by trailer, ready to be set on a foundation. In fact, there are even ways to move old, vintage houses from decaying neighborhoods or new-highway sites to the piece of property of your choice.

The advantages of considering all the kinds of housing available are several. You might find that you really can afford to get into something you own and considerably reduce your monthly housing costs. You might find that that charming old house on a quiet street in an old community you thought would be perfect won't be half as appealing, once you've looked at a condominium complex with an assortment of recreational facilities that fit your leisure activities exactly. The point is that you'll be cheating yourself if you don't take a good look at the variety of housing choices available in your chosen area before you make a decision. It's been said that being in the wrong house is like being in a bad marriage; you can always get out of it. Both, however, are likely to be costly and painful and to be avoided if possible.

The moral of the "just-looking" theory is that you might end up being happy with something totally different from your original, preconceived notion of your "dream." Just looking and talking with people who have chosen different types of housing, getting the feel of different types of communities, will not only give you more freedom of choice, it will give you more confidence in your final decision.

Old House Versus New House

The pros and cons of a new home versus an old home would be a good subject for debating teams, and if they were of equal skill, the debate would probably end in a draw. A pristine, never-lived-in-before, new home outfitted with air conditioning and modern mechanical (electric, heating, plumbing) systems and the latest model appliances represents a nice, clean slate on which you can, through your choice and yours alone, imprint your landscaping, your style, and your decor. An old home will have acquired a certain aura that is fondly called "charm," a heritage that you will acquire with it. A new home will have to go through a shakedown period; all the new systems might not work perfectly to start. An old home will be settled in its ways and have proven itself a workable place to live, but it might be due for a new roof or a new furnace or new plumbing. New home constructions may not have as soundproof walls as old ones, but they may have insulation that makes them far more energy-efficient than an old one. Because new homes are frequently built in developing areas, schools, churches, and shopping facilities may not yet be as established as they are in old-home communities. New homes, in a given development, may have small variety in their appearance as a result of assembly-

Today's home styling comes in a wide mixture of architectural styles. Most important in selecting a home is to choose a house that provides the kind of living best suited to you and your family. The four houses shown here represent, literally, different levels of living.

A ranch-style home has community living areas and sleeping areas all on one floor —with no stairs to climb. *Photo by Robert L. Beall for National Homes Manufacturing Company.*

This trilevel home has a fully finished basement which adds lots to the living space. *Photo by Robert L. Beall for National Homes Manufacturing Company.*

A bilevel home hugs the land and is great for unlevel terrain. Living quarters are separated into two levels by several steps instead of whole flights. *Photo by Robert L. Beall for National Homes Manufacturing Company.*

The two-story home provides a separation of family and communal living areas from sleeping quarters—great for privacy and late bed-makers. *Photo by Robert L. Beall for National Homes Manufacturing Company.*

line construction and design. Old homes often tend to more individuality, either in their original construction or in the additions they've undergone. One great advantage of a new development home is that it may require a smaller down payment than an old home. When builders are also the lenders, they will have gone into the money market to buy money for as many as a hundred or more mortgages. That they will get a better break than you can get as an individual borrower is evident. They're buying wholesale and you're buying retail.

However, the price of a new house is seldom subject to discussion. If an older house, after a thorough going-over by a building inspector, is found to be defective in some way, the price of the house may be expected to be adjusted accordingly.

New homes by an imaginative builder need not have a stamped-out, look-alike appearance. These homes, built in Houston, Texas, by Doyle Stuckey Homes, are only a small example of the variety possible.

This brand-new, old-style French, two-story house has a game room and two separate family living areas. *Photo courtesy of The Houston Post Company.*

This single-story contemporary home has three bedrooms and a family living area with a landscaped atrium. *Photo courtesy of The Houston Post Company.*

Four bedrooms, with a sitting room off the master bedroom, are only some of the features of this traditional-looking colonial. *Photo courtesy of The Houston Post Company.*

In the realty market, an old home is usually referred to as a "resale home." It sounds nicer than "used home." Many builders also run resale operations for homes that have been vacated in their developments. A resale house that is three to five years old might fairly be called a new-old house. Preferably it will have been through its shakedown period and had some landscaping,

When Betty and Dan Stewart moved into this 13-bedroom home built in 1890, they loved the high ceilings and the luxury of six fireplaces. Betty was able to incorporate an old oak cupboard they found in the pantry into her modern kitchen. *Photo by Robert Gonel.*

a mailbox, storm windows, and other accoutrements added. Many people look on these as a good buy, especially if the mortgage is available from the builder.

Whether you end up in an old house or a new one is just one of the eventual choices you'll make. Before you start the actual search for *the home*, you can narrow the field considerably by looking at the variety of home possibilities in your area. The point of this survey of your options is to look honestly at everything that's available to see how different homes suit your budget and how you feel about the kinds of homes and communities

In keeping with the gingerbread exterior of their home, the Stewarts found old wicker furniture and interior shutters for their living room. Son Nat has his own-sized wicker rocker. *Photo by Robert Gonel.*

This sturdy old home needed a great deal of refurbishing when Penny and Jim Armstrong bought it. Redo of the peeling stairs, plastering of cracked walls, and a multitude of small repairs turned it into a lovely, comfortable home. *Photo by Robert Gonel.*

This roomy old home provided more than enough living space for Shirley and Kendall Render and their two young children. The Renders' biggest job was a complete redo of all the painted woodwork and replacement of wallpaper throughout the house. *Photo by Robert Gonel.*

Old housing can have many different origins. When Betty and Warren Lucas went house hunting in North Salem, New York, in 1951, they were able to buy this old church for $3,000. The church was built in 1869, and had a cut-granite foundation. When the Lucases acquired it, they donated the pews to another church in Danbury, Connecticut, and went to work themselves to turn the building into a home. Betty remembers, "We borrowed a saw—we had a hammer —and we got started."

Five years later, the Lucases' home looked like this, and they had completed the major work of installing rooms in the building. Betty searched for furniture of good wood with good lines and did all the upholstery herself. "Today," she says, "people admire my antiques." *Photo by Cle Kinney.*

in which you find them. To start, talk to friends, become a follower of the real estate pages in your local paper, and, if necessary, knock on doors. After all, you are just looking, and most people will be happy to tell you what they like about where they live. Some may even volunteer what they don't like. You may not find all of these housing possibilities in the radius where your work dictates that you live, but give it a fair try.

A *traditional or conventionally built house* (referred to in the trade as a stick-built house) is one that has been built stone by stone or brick by brick or lumber by lumber on its site. These homes can be found in a great variety of communities, from isolated one-time farms to small towns to newly developed hous-

The exterior of the 1,200-square-foot, two-story house that Gedney and Patricia Howe bought and restored themselves in Charleston, South Carolina. Purchased for $22,000 in 1973, it was sold five years—and countless hours of work later—for $70,000. *Photo by Amos S. Jones*

ing communities to older areas in cities. This is the category in which you'll find the greatest variety of styles, locations, and that elusive quality, ambience.

Try to explore at least three or four quite different locations. You'll not only get the feel of different settings, but you'll begin to get some knowledge about the dollar value of different homes. An older home in a country setting with a few acres of land may cost about the same as a new home on a half-acre lot in a housing development, but you won't really know how you respond to each setting until you experience it.

Visit at least one new housing development. There you can look at a model home and often there will be brochures avail-

After the Howes sold their first home, they purchased this old, uncared-for, 24,000-square-foot home, known in Charleston as "the Calhoun Mansion." Its purchase price: $200,000. They lived in one room for 18 months while restoration was being done on the 15-bedroom house. But such beautiful features as solid walnut wainscotting, a music room with a vaulted skylight, and domed, handpainted ceilings made it all worthwhile.

Carpenters worked for 8 months to restore and repair the home's porch columns. As painters add finishing touches Gedney Howe, III, inspects, new plantings. *Photo by The Charleston News and Courier.*

The Calhoun Mansion today. *Photo by Ernest Ferguson.*

able, showing the variety of styles a builder plans for the community.

Look at older homes in a small town. Towns tend to provide closer neighbors, an established community of activities, and perhaps less privacy than you're seeking.

Look in an established housing development where there may be homes for resale. If you want to look at houses that are listed with a real estate agent, don't hesitate to do it now, but do let the agent know that you are in the process of looking around. A realtor with a long-range point of view will usually be willing to direct you to a variety of possibilities, and may ask some helpful questions about your needs and preferences that will help you zero in on your wants.

City single-family housing has appealed to a great many young first-home buyers. This kind of city housing is found in older neighborhoods where the move is to restore or renovate or rehabilitate old homes that have been neglected. The appeal is in the space acquired and in the challenge of doing a great deal of the refurbishing work yourself. Also, there are often funds available through city programs to help finance the restoration or provide low mortgage-interest rates, and the size of the home makes it possible to gain a rental income from a portion of the house during the early years of the restoration work. (See Chapter 4 for more information on this.)

Peggy Wall is in charge of the Urban Revitalization Program of the National Home Builders Association. She warns that the move to a really old urban dwelling can be "the ultimate test of a marriage." She recommends that it can only be done if a kitchen and one room are liveable before moving in.

If patience is one of your virtues and you really enjoy stripping old wallpaper off walls and layers of paint off a balustrade, as Cathi and Travis Hemlepp had to do in their Park Slope home in Brooklyn, this kind of housing deserves your exploration. Some of the jobs people tackled seemed endless. Tom Gottshall said he never wanted to see peeling paint again after he burned the old lead paint off nineteen porch columns and 282 spindels of his Columbia, South Carolina, home.

However, all of the people we talked with who had chosen really old homes were delighted with their projects.

Manufactured houses, as opposed to stick-built houses, come in a far greater variety of styles, sizes, and prices than you may have thought, and you will find them in a wider variety of communities today. The term "manufactured house" refers to a home that has either been built and finished in a factory, such as a mobile home, or to homes that have been prefabricated to some degree in a factory, then shipped and assembled on a home site. Prefabricated housing has a long history. The first one in America was shipped from England to be erected on Cape Ann in the seventeenth century. In 1830, a beautiful prefabricated home was floated down the river from Ohio to Natchez, Missis-

Brownstones everywhere are treasured for their space and, often, for the treasures they house such as old lighting fixtures, solid wood balustrades, and beautiful wood floors. Some owners choose to restore. Some choose to modernize, as architect Peter Samtom did in his old New York home shown here. *Photo by David Hirsch.*

If you can't find an old barn to renovate, you can buy one ready-to-build. This home, shown under construction, is only one of the many styles available. The simple, popular barn design combines old timbers with modern construction methods, and within the basic structure, rooms or lofts can be incorporated according to the owner's needs and wishes. Design by Emil Hanslin. *Photo courtesy Yankee Barn Homes.*

sippi, and in the early part of this century Sears Roebuck's "Honor-Bilt" mail-order homes were shipped throughout the country.

Unfortunately, manufactured housing has struggled against two images that are outmoded by today's standards. Mobile homes are judged to be the boxy occupants of trailer parks, and prefabricated homes are remembered as the not-too-inspired designs that emerged during World War II. Quite a lot has happened since then in the manufactured-home industry, and it is an alternative that has attracted a great many young first-home buyers, especially those who are planning to build on their own land, or those who plan to do some of the work on their homes themselves.

Manufactured homes come in a variety of degrees of finishing. *"Panelized" or pre-engineered* homes are assembled in wall

This lovely, two-story, traditional Tudor is also a manufactured home. What's meant by a manufactured home is that all or part of the house is precut and produced, and shipped in a package or kit—depending on what the individual manufacturer calls it—to the site. There it is erected by a contractor if it's complicated, a do-it-yourselfer if it's simple, or by both, each doing what they do best. *Photo courtesy of Pease Company.*

panels at the factory and pieced together at the building site. Panelized homes offer literally hundreds of designs, and the panels can be arranged in a variety of ways to suit the size and shape of the lot. Manufacturers of panelized homes do not claim that their products cost less than a stick-built house (prices range up to $250,000, exclusive of land). They feel, however, that they are able to exercise greater control of materials than many local builders because they buy in great quantities rather than from local lumber dealers. Also, because of precision machinery used in the factory, prefabricated-housing manufacturers feel they have greater carpentry controls than in many stick-built houses. There is also a time advantage in acquiring a new prefabricated house, especially the panelized models. One manufacturer gives its builders a one-day schedule to erect the shell of a 1,200-square-foot house. They estimate it would take ten days to get a

This ranch house with two-car garage is actually a manufactured home— what they used to call a "prefab." Today, they come in the widest variety of styles imaginable, with options both inside and out to suit the individual buyer. *Photo courtesy of Harvest Homes.*

The Jeffersonian is the name for this stately, spacious manufactured home. The advantage of the manufactured home, whether you do it yourself or not—and some you simply can't—is that they go up much more quickly than the start-from-scratch variety. All or most of the materials are right there, and you don't have to wait for special orders to come in. *Photo courtesy of Scholz Homes, Inc.*

This entryway to a mobile/manufactured home comes as a surprise to people who remember when such structures were simply "trailers," and were used largely by traveling vacationers. *Photo courtesy of Association of Manufactured Homes.*

The Shenandoah looks like a genuine antique on the outside, but it's really a manufactured bilevel dwelling. Some makers of manufactured houses actually reproduce classic old architecture down to the smallest detail. *Photo courtesy of Scholz Homes, Inc.*

Log houses are among the most popular of manufactured homes for do-it-yourself-ers. Usually, owners have the foundation laid by a professional. The kit or package includes everything necessary to construct the home. Users have declared the instructions and numbered pieces are easy to follow and put together. *Photo courtesy of New England Log Homes.*

stick-built house to the same degree of completion. The speed of construction not only cuts down on the likelihood of theft of materials, but allows construction to continue in spite of bad weather.

Precut and numbered lumber packages are another form of prefabricated home. All carpentry is done at the site. This is an option for ambitious do-it-yourselfers. When David and Vicky Caroline decided to move out of their apartment in North Branford, Connecticut, they couldn't find a home that suited both of them. They ordered a log-cabin type of package home from New England Log Homes. "It was fairly easy to construct," explained David, "following the step-by-step guide supplied with

Log houses were once strictly vacation homes, but now folks throughout the country are choosing them as primary dwellings. *Photo courtesy of New England Log Homes.*

the package. We love the house and it's something to be proud of because I built it myself."

In your search, you may find erected prefabricated homes in new developments or you may find them on a street between

The owners of this warm, cozy, log house say they love the ease of upkeep—especially the absence of plastered and painted interior walls to keep clean. *Photo courtesy of New England Log Homes.*

site-built homes, and you might never know which was which. The way you judge a prefabricated house should be as you judge any other house, not with a preconception your parents might hold.

Modular homes are manufactured in units that have all the pipes, fixtures, bathrooms, kitchens, and flooring installed at the factory. These are shipped in two or more units and bolted together at the site. There is less room for customizing and less design variety in the modular homes than in other types of prefabricated homes. These differ from mobile homes only in that they are built to a different construction code.

Until recently, *mobile homes,* have usually been located on an owner's property or in land-rental developments known as parks. The old idea of a mobile home as a recreational vehicle has been fast disappearing, and about 98 percent of the mobile homes produced are never moved farther than to their original site. The great advantage of the mobile home is its affordability. In 1979, the price range on a new mobile home was from $8,000 to $50,000, exclusive of land. The average single-wide home (about 966 square feet) sold for $13,000, and the average multi-section (about 1,440 square feet) for $20,350.

A well-run mobile-home rental park resembles an attractive suburban development with well-lit streets, sidewalks with curbs and gutters, off-street parking, a clubhouse, and recreational facilities such as a swimming pool, tennis courts, and basketball courts.

In 1976, Sherry and Bob Eberhardt faced a rising rental on their one-bedroom apartment and despaired of finding housing they could afford with their $1,000 savings. They eventually bought a four-year-old, single-wide mobile home in Chantilly, Virginia, for $6,000 with a 20 percent down payment and a little help from Sherry's parents. Their monthly mortgage, lot rent, and utilities came to a little less than the rent they were paying. In 1978, after their child was born, they sold their first house for $8,500 and bought a double-wide home for $14,000. "One day," Bob added, "we'll probably get a house on land of our own."

The newest development in mobile home planning has resulted from relaxed zoning laws in several states that allow mobile homes to be situated in a typical housing development and treated for tax purposes and financing as conventional real estate. In Montgomery County, Maryland, one such development, operated by Berk Enterprises, offers only double-wide homes in four styles, priced from $40,000 to $50,000, including the land, which Gary Nordheimer of Berk estimates at 20 percent of the home value.

Multifamily dwellings that offer ownership are becoming increasingly available in both old and new housing. Old double or two-family homes are looked upon as prize possessions, and you

This double-wide mobile-manufactured home is on a quiet street in the Virginia suburbs of Washington, D.C. All utility lines in this community are underground. *Photo courtesy of Association of Manufactured Homes.*

The roomy interior of a double-section, mobile/manufactured shelter is home to a young couple who work in Washington, D.C. *Photo courtesy of National Association of Manufactured Homes.*

may be lucky to find one because they provide such an obvious rental income to help with the financing of the home. But in new building and the conversion of old housing, cooperative apartments and condominiums are providing an extremely popular housing choice: the financial advantages of owning your home with none of the responsibilities of such upkeep as yard care, exterior repairs, and the like.

With co-ops, a lot of your monthly maintenance charges can be deducted from your taxes since such charges do include mortgage interest, real estate taxes, and, of course, necessary maintenance. And because all maintenance considered necessary is paid for—whereas the single-family house dweller will frequently do for himself at little or no cost—there are some savings to be had here, too. Also, co-ops, as you'll soon learn, are corporations—which may make a difference in your tax savings as well. With condominiums, conditions are so much more variable, there is no rule-of-thumb concerning tax savings. Most people we talked to warned us that all agreements should be read very carefully, and that you should have all questions answered very thoroughly.

A *condominium* is a home you own in a multi-unit building. It may be an apartmentlike complex or it may be a town house or a unit in cluster housing. You are the sole owner of the inner space or rooms described in your title and, in conjunction with all the other owners in the complex, you own a share of the common grounds, recreational facilities, and any other amenities that are part of the complex, such as a sauna. As a condominium owner, you are responsible for the upkeep of your interior space and you contribute a monthly fee for the upkeep of the commonly held elements. Thomas Seldin, a builder in Omaha, Nebraska, has built such a complex in the outer, suburban growth area of Omaha. A two-bedroom apartment there cost $24,950 in 1979. The maintenance fee for that facility was then $39 per month, up from $32 per month five years previously. The maintenance is paid into the Owners' Association, but as the owner of the inner space, you are responsible for your own financing and you get your own tax bill. If you have any

Cluster housing that can be either cooperative- or condominium-owned appeals to many people who want to share the responsibilities of home ownership and care. This 124-unit apartment village in Fullerton, California, has five recreational areas. Plazas, fountains, and trees dot the landscape. *Photo from Clay Publicom.*

Condominimum housing is fast meeting the needs of young couples who want living space of their own. This modern structure in Omaha, Nebraska, has two-bedroom apartments that sold for $24,950 in early 1979 and carried a maintenance charge of $39 per month. *Photo Courtesy of Seldin Development and Management Co.*

Two-bedroom apartments in this more traditional condominium also sell for about $25,000 in Omaha. The homes are located near shopping centers and are near all major bus lines into the city. *Photo courtesy of Seldin Development and Management Co.*

These multifamily homes, set well apart on wide, paved streets, were precut, partially assembled in a factory, and shipped to the building site to be erected. Their design and construction allow for a great feeling of privacy and space. *Photo courtesy of Kingsberry Homes, Boise Cascade Corporation.*

doubts about your willingness to mow a lawn or to be a putterer around the house, look at a condominium as a possible life-style that would appeal to you.

Cooperative apartments differ from condominiums in their form of ownership. A cooperative is owned by a corporation and, as an occupant, you own stock in that corporation, which entitles you to live in a specified unit or apartment. A cooperative has a board of directors who can decide whether or not, and to whom, you can sell your apartment and what interior changes you can make. Because the cooperative is paying the taxes and the mortgage interest on the building, your tax deduction will be alloted according to the number of shares you own. In a cooperative you can get your own financing, although in a builder cooperative the builder may offer financing. There is a monthly maintenance fee in a cooperative. Always ask about it, and par-

This fun structure is made for sunshine (note the solar-heating panels on the roof), although it's pretty cozy when the snows fly, too. Good manufactured design for vacation or for primary dwelling.   *Photo courtesy of Acorn Structures.*

ticularly ask about how fast it has been rising. Old cooperative buildings that have needed substantial capital improvement may have high monthly maintenance charges.

Then there's always the choice of *building your own home.* This takes not a little time and skill and a long-range point of view. In the trade, this effort is called "sweat equity" and many young couples have chosen it as a method of acquiring a home. Often, however, they've chosen to do only the work they've felt equipped to handle and to that extent saved some money. Some acted as their own general contractors and saved 15 percent to 25 percent of the house cost. Some went to school to learn how to do their own plumbing or wiring. Others went to schools such as the Shelter Institute in Bath, Maine, which teaches, in a fifteen-week evening course, how to build a home. Even then, most chose to have a good foundation laid by a hired, experienced hand. *Warning:* there are local codes for wiring and plumbing. Check at your town offices to find out the requirements.

Many people relied on some form of *manufactured home* when they decided to invest their time and work in a housebuilding project. Some producers of precut homes ship the components to the site and have their crews put up the shell on the owner's foundation. They then deliver the interior materials and systems, including paint and appliances, and store them inside the shell. How much work the owner-builder does and how much is hired done will influence the amount of money saved.

When Debby and Paul Holmes couldn't find a home they liked —they were hoping for a contemporary home in the old New England town of Hingham, Massachusetts—they asked Paul's father, a designer, to plan one for them. Then Paul and Debby went to work on their three-story, cathedral-ceiling home. One of Debby's acquaintances observed, "She's just one of those people who can do anything." (Debby is now the first woman police officer in Hingham.) The Holmeses had the masonry, electric, and plumbing systems installed by professionals. Paul did such things as interior walls by himself, and admits that he's got some sheet-rock seams that are cracked and need repair and that he needs to install a new kitchen floor. But overall, they're happy with their home.

Steven Smith in Hamersville, Ohio, started to build his contemporary home when he was a bachelor. He said, "I guess it was just a family tradition. My father had built his home years ago." Steve started with an advantage—he's an architect—and designed the home himself to be built in two stages. He lived in an apartment and worked on the house for two and a half years before he moved in in 1975. He and his new wife, Glenna, now occupy the completed house.

Of such a project, one owner-builder said, "It takes a long time. You have to be committed."

On the following pages you will find a set of Home Option sheets to record your impressions as you're "just looking." You'll be judging more specifically when you get down to serious business.

Note: If you are interested in a precut or panelized manufactured house, send to the National Association of Home Manufacturers, 6521 Arlington Boulevard, Falls Church, VA 22012 for *A Guide to Manufactured Homes,* a $4 brochure that is a good introduction to the homes and lists names of manufacturers from whom you can get catalogues.

For information about mobile and modular homes, write to the Manufactured Housing Institute, 1745 Jefferson Highway, Arlington, VA 22202. Ask for the name and address of the director of your State Mobile Homes Association. He can give you information on dealers, parks, and developments in your area.

This charming Cape Cod Bow House comes as a kit with hand-blown glass window panes, 12-inch wide pine floor boards, cut nails and old-fashioned storm windows. Do-it-yourselfers often have manufactured panels put in place by a builder, then do most of the finishing work themselves to save as much as possible on their housing costs. *Photo courtesy of Bow House Inc.*

3

The Search for a Home

When the seventeenth-century religious poet George Herbert observed that "the buyer needs a hundred eyes, the seller not one," he was speaking in proverbial generality, but he might well have been referring to the purchase of a home. Two of our interviewees said the same thing in modern-day language. From Donna Johnson: "You'll always find more than meets the eye" (remember that the Johnsons moved into a home that was waterless). And from Walter Sosnowski: "Nothing is ever what it appears to be. No matter how much you measure and how much you look, you never know what's there for sure until you move in."

If these sound like the same warning signals you read in the opening chapter of this book, they are. Experienced home buyers warn that it's all too easy to become enchanted and excited when you find a house you like at a price you can afford. As one buyer told us, "You're so sure this house is for you that you only see the things you like. Everything else glazes out. It's a little like falling in love."

Perhaps that analogy is a fair one. Just as you know that a perfect person does not exist, you'll hear or read over and over again that the perfect house does not exist. Pursuing your initial attraction until you're sure the faults are ones you can live with, and the decision to seal the bargain is one you've given enough objective evaluation to, are good criteria for any long-term commitment. While choosing a home is your investment and your final decision, there is help available—and it's especially advisable if this is your first home-buying foray.

HELP WANTED

By now you've got a pretty good idea of about where you'd like to live, what type of home you would like to consider, and how much you can afford to spend. It's time to zero in on all the help you can get to find the place that most nearly matches your wants.

Become Your Own Best-Read Friend

If you haven't already become a follower of real estate news, now is the time to dip into it. Business-oriented national magazines, news weeklies, and large metropolitan newspapers report what's happening in the real estate market. Like any other market, it fluctuates. At times it is fiercely competitive, and at other times there are homes going wanting for buyers. One dramatic example of the changing market took place in Orange County, California, in the years 1978–1979. In the spring of 1978, housing was so tight that lotteries were being run to determine who would win the lucky number and, with it, the privilege of buying a home. By the spring of 1979, there was a housing surplus and builders were offering potential buyers such inducements as free draperies, fences, air conditioning, backyard "hot tubs," and, in one instance, mortgages at 9 percent interest, well below the going rate of 10½ percent. Knowing the rate of the market when you go into it can give you a better idea of your chances of finding a bargain or evaluating your position in price negotiations.

Checklist 2d. OLD HOMES WE'VE SEEN

Description	Address	Surroundings	Impressions Favorable or Unfavorable

Checklist 2e. NEW HOMES WE'VE SEEN

Description	Address	Surroundings	Impressions Favorable or Unfavorable

Checklist 2f. CONDOMINIUMS WE'VE SEEN

Description	Address	Surroundings	Impressions Favorable or Unfavorable

Checklist 2g. COOPERATIVES WE'VE SEEN

Description	Address	Surroundings	Impressions Favorable or Unfavorable

Checklist 2h. HOMES WE'VE LOOKED AT TO PUT ON OUR LAND

Description	Address	Surroundings	Impressions Favorable or Unfavorable

At the same time, start reading real estate ads. They will give you an idea of prices being asked for the kind of home you'd like to buy. Also, you'll get an idea of the kinds of homes and the price range handled by different real estate agencies. Most large daily newspapers have large listings once a week, frequently on weekends. Some of the metropolitan papers have separate suburban sections. If you haven't yet decided which suburban area you'd like to live in, you can get the variety of sections by going directly to the newspaper office. If you have decided fairly certainly on the area you'd like, it'll be worthwhile to subscribe to a local community newspaper. You may spot an owner-advertised house that's just what you're looking for. Also, it's much easier to sift through the local newspaper listings than the forbiddingly long listings in metropolitan papers. In addition to newspapers, small booklets listing homes for sale are often available at no charge at drugstores, newsstands, sometimes in supermarkets. These are paid for by local builders and real estate firms. They too can give you an idea of the offerings in that community.

A word of warning about ads: Beware the descriptive adjectives. "Prestigious, historic, fabulous, scenic, lovely"—they're all words designed to lure you to a given house. For example, if you peeled the adjectives out of this house ad that appeared in a New York newspaper in the spring of 1979, you'd have an ordinary three-bedroom house with a living room, dining room, kitchen, and finished basement. This is how the ad read (in part): "BIG! BOLD! BRICK and BEAUTIFUL This breathtaking home can be yours for only. . . . Luxurious living room, banquet-sized dining room, miracle kitchen, 3 master bedrooms PLUS Disco 54 finished basement playroom. Fantastic area. Remember, all this glorious living can be yours for only $244 a month." Charming doll houses, productive "farmettes," and gorgeous, rambling ranches all deserve to be read about with a questioning mind.

Tell Your Friends Who Own One

People who have been through the home-buying experience will be sympathetic to your quest, and often know about friends of theirs who are moving and likely to have a house for sale. Here again, if you're planning to buy in an area you know, tell the local tradespeople, including the ad salesman or editor of the local newspaper. Enlist neighbors and acquaintances. They may drive a different route than you do, and can direct you to some "for sale" signs they've spotted. Speak to people where you work and give them an idea of what you're looking for. If you're house hunting (as opposed to condominium or cooperative hunting), try to enlist the help of some older friends or acquaintances. They may know contemporaries who are planning to move into a smaller home or an apartment and are ready to sell their present home.

Go See Owner-Advertised Houses and Attend "Open Houses"

If you end up buying a house directly from an owner, you may save some money. The seller always pays the real estate agent's fee (5 percent to 8 percent of the cost of the house), but that amount is usually added to the owner's asking price—so you, the buyer, actually pay part, if not all, of that fee. When you deal with an owner directly, you do deprive yourself of a great deal of knowledge and help that a good realtor can provide, so any savings may be questionable. The main advantage of talking with home owners and attending open houses in the early stages of your search is that you will get a more direct feel for the people and the community. Don't, at this stage—no matter how much you love a house—sign any papers or put any money down. There's a lot more to know and a lot more help you'll need before formalizing any transaction. You can express a verbal interest in the house and promise you'll be back in touch with the owners within a reasonable length of time. Then race home and finish this chapter of the book *plus* chapters 4 and 5. You don't want to lose a house you love, but neither do you want to buy a house without full knowledge of its value.

*   *   *

Consult Several Real Estate Agents or Brokers

If you can, choose those who are listed as realtors. They are members of the National Association of Realtors and conform to the association's established code of ethics. Even though you are not the person responsible for paying the realtor, he or she will be interested in helping you find what you want because there's no commission until a house is sold. You may have to shop around to find an agent who hears what you want and has such a home among the firm's listings. Do your part by communicating fairly with the agent about the price range you can handle and being specific about the kind of home you want.

Don't be dismayed if, for one reason or another, the first real estate agent you contact doesn't have anything to show you. The Mitilieris remember that they called on an agent who handled real estate in the Annandale section of Staten Island, and told her they wanted a two-family house in the $50,000 to $52,000 price range. She laughed and said. "There's nothing." She'd have been a better agent had she omitted the laugh. Don't be put off by an agent who is unfriendly or doesn't seem understanding. They are people and you are people, and it's your job and your right to find someone you like and trust.

Donna and Norm Johnson started out with eight or nine agents and, as they narrowed the geographic field and learned who was showing them what they wanted, they ended up dealing with only two.

When Freddi and Bob Greenberg went house hunting in the Bedford–Pound Ridge–Chappaqua area north of New York City, they had two musts: *not* a split-level ranch-style and *not* a house near a busy road. Freddi recalls, "Fifty split-level ranch-styles later, I really got firm with that agent and told her not to call us to show us one more ranch house and *nothing* on a highway. We almost lost the house we got because it is fairly near to a busy road, but it's in a cul-de-sac and we don't get traffic noise. I think I frightened the agent."

When you find an agent with whom you communicate well and one who represents a reputable firm, you will have a lot more than just someone who shows you a house. A good agent will know the housing market in general. He'll know what properties are available in his area at what prices. He may know something about the history of the house. He'll be familiar with zoning laws, neighborhood values, the value of the homes you're looking at as long-term investments or their resale value. He will be familiar with real estate lawyers, building inspectors, and real estate appraisers.

Be selective about the firm, then find the person who senses your needs and stick with that person. Remember, however, that houses are often listed with several real estate firms. You are committed to deal with whoever showed you the house first so you should shop carefully for a realtor before you start your search. Ask friends, people where you work, tradespeople. Ask how long the firm has been in business. Is it headed by a realtor? Check recommended firms' advertising. Do they run ads regularly? Full-time agencies will; part-timers may not. Do their listings vary from week to week or do they seem to repeat themselves? Varied listings indicate a broader range of houses and a better turnover. Repeat listings usually mean slow-moving houses and possibly a small selection of houses.

As you shop for realtors, you will find that some firms belong to a nationally advertised conglomerate. The advantage of dealing with such a firm, according to one realtor, is that they have access to listings over a broad geographic area. The disadvantage, according to an independent realtor, is that the agent's fee is less when it has to be split with the parent firm, so that the conglomerate agent may not give you as much of his time and attention as an independent agent would.

On Checklist 3a, start an evaluation of real estate agents. You may find you'll want to add to these or eliminate some when you narrow down your list of possible neighborhoods.

LOCATING THE RIGHT NEIGHBORHOOD

There's an old adage in the real estate business that says, "The three most important things to look for in a home are location, location, and location." Certainly the first of those important locations is the neighborhood—what it's like now and what it's going to be. The choice of a neighborhood will affect you and your family in three extremely important ways: (1) your current budget, (2) the compatibility you'll find among the people and present life-style of the community, and (3) the future resale value of your home. It's crucial to your happiness that the location of the home you eventually choose please both your person and your purse.

Your house-ad reading and your discussions with real estate agents will begin to lead you to communities that offer the kind of home you want in the price range you can afford. Just as soon as you feel you've narrowed the choices down to two or three neighborhoods, take at least one day for serious investigation of each area. This is a job to do on your own, *not* with a real estate agent, unless you feel he or she can provide *all* the correct answers. Take along a trusted friend if you like; two pairs of eyes are always better than one. If a family is involved, all the principals should be on this trip, but consider leaving small children with a sitter. There's a lot to do and see in one day. Plan your trip on a day when responsible city or town or county officials are in their offices. It can wreck your best-laid plans if there's no one on duty except a receptionist to answer phones or, worse still, the offices are closed for the day.

First, research the questions that will affect your budget. The first question in that category is *property taxes*. If you've looked at specific homes with your real estate agent, he will be able to tell you what the property taxes have been on those houses. If you haven't looked at specific houses, you can find out how houses of the type you would like to buy are assessed. But just as important as the current tax bite is how fast the property taxes have been rising. Check out the increases in the past five to ten years. Also, ask whether the property is usually reevaluated when ownership changes hands. Will your property taxes be more than the previous owner's? While you're talking with town officials, ask what the property taxes cover. Low taxes might simply mean poor services, like a bad school system, an inadequate police force, indifferent care of roads, and so on down the line.

At the same time you're checking property taxes, ask about any *special assessments* that might affect your budget. Is a new bond issue in the offing for a community improvement? Have new tax rates been issued for the coming year? Town officials should be able and willing to answer these questions. But you should ask further in the area where you plan to buy if there are neighborhood organizations you will be expected to join and to which you will be expected to contribute for improvement projects. Before you leave the town official's office ask about zoning in the community (see later in this section for more on zoning regulations).

While you can't get a specific figure until you are evaluating a given home, you can ask about average *utility bills* for the type of home you plan to buy. Also ask how fast these rates have been rising in the last five years. They're a cost to be reckoned with. Another specific you can't get at until later is heating costs, but you can ask friends or people you meet in the neighborhood how heating fuel costs have been running. Expect that these costs, too, are on the increase.

Check out *commutation costs* accurately. Expect that these are costs that will also be rising. Whether you plan to use private or public transportation, it's a necessary expense to add to the monthly outlay. While the reliability of the public transportation won't necessarily affect your budget, it can certainly affect your state of mind. Get the price from the transport system, but check the reliability with people who have used it.

If your budgetary exploration hasn't turned up any forbidding costs, go ahead and check out the following characteristics of the neighborhood that will affect your family and your life-style:

Schools may not be important to your present or future plans, but if you have children, schools will be of primary importance. You might start by visiting with the superintendent of schools and the president of the local PTA. The superintendent, if he is proud of his system, should be willing to tell you how his students rate in achievement tests as compared to the average state

Checklist 3a. REAL ESTATE AGENTS

Agency name   1. _____

Address   _____

Telephone number   _____

Agent we saw   _____

Agency name   2. _____

Address   _____

Telephone number   _____

Agent we saw   _____

Agency name   3. _____

Address   _____

Telephone number   _____

Agent we saw   _____

Agency name   4. _____

Address   _____

Telephone number   _____

Agent we saw   _____

Agency name   5. _____

Address   _____

Telephone number   _____

Agent we saw   _____

Checklist 3b. EVALUATION OF REAL ESTATE AGENCIES
("yes" answers are the best indicators)

Agencies	1	2	3	4	5
Is agency headed by a realtor?					
Does agency have several listings in our price range?					
Has agency been in business more than 5 years?					
Does agency advertise regularly?					
Do agency listings change with regularity?					
Does agent seem interested in what we need?					
Is agent showing us what we're looking for?					
Does agent seem knowledgeable about the real estate market?					
Does agent seem knowledgeable about local property taxes?					
Does agent seem willing to tell us what's right and what's wrong with the house?					
Is the agent knowledgeable about the neighborhood?					
Do you like and trust the agent?					

NOTES

scores. He should be willing to tell you the college placement records of his graduating classes, how much money is spent per pupil, and how that compares to the state averages. Through the PTA president, you can get the names of some parents who have children your children's ages. Try to talk to several of them and to the children themselves, to get their evaluation of the schools and the teachers. Discuss with the PTA head how much change has taken place in the schools in the past ten years. Is the school administration open to new facilities and teaching techniques? Eventually, you'll want to visit some actual classes with your children.

Even if you don't have, or plan to have, children, ask in a more general way about the community schools. They are an indication of the community's commitment to its citizens. However, all other things being equal, if you don't have any need for good schools, you might find a neighboring town without an expensive school system just as desirable and with much lower property taxes.

Recreation facilities and clubs can be important both to you and your children. A good *hospital* or *medical center* for reliable emergency care is valuable for your peace of mind. So are an efficient *police force* and *fire department*.

Stop into a *shopping center* and note the variety of stores as well as the prices. Locate the *churches* you might choose to attend. Stop into the local Chamber of Commerce and get a list of the *clubs* that function in that community. They may have a great deal of literature that can make interesting reading when you get home. Remember that it's been professionally designed to sell the glories of the community. They may also provide you with a good map of the city or town.

Community zoning regulations will not only affect your own plans for the property you buy, but will give you a clue to the regulations that affect the town and any undeveloped property within the town limits. Ask to see the master plans for the community. They will tell you a lot about the prospects for the future growth and character of the town.

Check to be sure zoning regulations prohibit commercial establishments in residential sections. A beer parlor in your block could decrease the value of your home enormously. On the other hand, be sure the regulations don't prohibit you from having something you've always wanted. Fences bordering property, for example, or adding a second story to a house, are not permitted in some communities. So if it's a picket fence you've always longed for, or a cute little dormer, think again.

This is a good time to ask whether the community is growing and whether the real estate values have been rising. Ask too about the crime rate. These are all objective statistics and not opinions. They should constitute reliable information, but if you have any doubt about the answers, keep asking the same questions of others.

Water supply, sewage disposal, and *garbage disposal* may be part of the town services. Check to see if they are adequate and if they satisfactorily meet the community's needs.

Look back to your own personal wants (Checklist 1c). Is there an educational facility nearby for your own continuing education? Are there enough tennis courts at a reasonable price if tennis is your thing?

Once you've got the facts, spend some time just driving around looking at the community, its homes, streets, and shops. Talk to as many people as you can. You're looking now for subjective judgments, how you feel about this community as a place to live. Be aware of the traffic and the people on the streets. What's it like at ten in the morning, at noon, at nine or ten at night? If you haven't already done it, take out a short subscription to the local newspaper. In metropolitan areas, there are often weekly neighborhood papers that are quite different in character from the large dailies. You'll be surprised how differently you'll look at the paper after you've made a study of the community.

Using Checklist 3c, record your findings of the day.

Checklist 3c. LOCATING THE RIGHT NEIGHBORHOOD

Community or development #1

Name_____

Areas we like best _____

_____

_____

Budget considerations (enter annual costs)
Property taxes (estimated) $_____

Special assessments likely   _____

New bond issues passed or proposed   _____

Utility costs (estimated)   _____

Heating costs (estimated—in warm climates
consider extra cost of air conditioning if needed)   _____

Commutation costs (include all workers and school
bus charges for children)   _____

Other certain costs of living in neighborhood
(individually paid garbage disposal, neighborhood
improvement projects, etc.)   _____

Total Cost of Living in Neighborhood
(over and above mortgage payments) $_____

Note: Rate of property tax rise (last 5 yrs.)   _____%

Rate of utility cost rise (last 5 yrs.)   _____%

Rate of heating fuel cost rise (last 5 yrs.)   _____%

Rate of commuter cost rise (last 5 years)   _____%

Checklist 3d. THE COMMUNITY

Community or development #1
(Rate on a scale of 1 to 3: 1 = excellent, 2 = good, 3 = fair; no rating speaks for itself)

	1	2	3
School system			
Hospital or medical center			
Police protection			
Air pollution controls			
Water quality and quantity			
Sanitary disposal system			
Trash and garbage disposal			
Streets (quiet, cleanliness, lighting)			
Shopping facilities			
Church availability			
Car parking space or garage			
Recreational facilities			
Local public transportation			
Commutation system			
Zoning regulations and/or master plan			

General impression: Write in here how you reacted to the appearance and character of the neighborhood and how you felt about the people you met and talked to. Note particularly if you observed any objectionable smells or noises.

_____

_____

_____

_____

Checklist 3c. LOCATING THE RIGHT NEIGHBORHOOD

Community or development #2

Name_____

Areas we like best _____

_____

_____

Budget considerations (enter annual costs)
Property taxes (estimated) $_____

Special assessments likely   _____

New bond issues passed or proposed   _____

Utility costs (estimated)   _____

Heating costs (estimated—in warm climates
    consider extra cost of air conditioning if needed)   _____

Commutation costs (include all workers and school
    bus charges for children)   _____

Other certain costs of living in neighborhood
    (individually paid garbage disposal, neighborhood
    improvement projects, etc.)   _____

Total Cost of Living in Neighborhood (over and above
    mortgage payments) $_____

Note: Rate of property tax rise (last 5 yrs.)   _____%

Rate of utility cost rise (last 5 yrs.)   _____%

Rate of heating fuel cost rise (last 5 yrs.)   _____%

Rate of commuter cost rise (last 5 years)   _____%

Checklist 3d. THE COMMUNITY

Community or development #2
(Rate on a scale of 1 to 3: 1 = excellent, 2 = good, 3 = fair; no rating speaks for itself)

	1	2	3
School system			
Hospital or medical center			
Police protection			
Air pollution controls			
Water quality and quantity			
Sanitary disposal system			
Trash and garbage disposal			
Streets (quiet, cleanliness, lighting)			
Shopping facilities			
Church availability			
Car parking space or garage			
Recreational facilities			
Local public transportation			
Commutation system			
Zoning regulations and/or master plan			

General impression: Write in here how you reacted to the appearance and character of the neighborhood and how you felt about the people you met and talked to. Note particularly if you observed any objectionable smells or noises.

Checklist 3c. LOCATING THE RIGHT NEIGHBORHOOD

Community or development #3

Name_____

Areas we like best _____

_____

_____

Budget considerations (enter annual costs)
  Property taxes (estimated) $_____

  Special assessments likely   _____

  New bond issues passed or proposed   _____

  Utility costs (estimated)   _____

  Heating costs (estimated—in warm climates
    consider extra cost of air conditioning if needed) _____

Commutation costs (include all workers and school
bus charges for children)   _____

Other certain costs of living in neighborhood
(individually paid garbage disposal, neighborhood
improvement projects, etc.)   _____

Total Cost of Living in Neighborhood (over and above
  mortgage payments) $_____

Note: Rate of property tax rise (last 5 yrs.)   _____%

      Rate of utility cost rise (last 5 yrs.)   _____%

      Rate of heating fuel cost rise (last 5 yrs.)   _____%

      Rate of commuter cost rise (last 5 years)   _____%

Checklist 3d. THE COMMUNITY

(Rate on a scale of 1 to 3: 1 = excellent, 2 = good, 3 = fair; no rating speaks for itself)

	1	2	3
School system			
Hospital or medical center			
Police protection			
Air pollution controls			
Water quality and quantity			
Sanitary disposal system			
Trash and garbage disposal			
Streets (quiet, cleanliness, lighting)			
Shopping facilities			
Church availability			
Car parking space or garage			
Recreational facilities			
Local public transportation			
Commutation system			
Zoning regulations and/or master plan			

General impression: Write in here how you reacted to the appearance and character of the neighborhood and how you felt about the people you met and talked to. Note particularly if you observed any objectionable smells or noises.

_____

_____

_____

_____

_____

HOW TO JUDGE ANY HOUSE

Armed with a selection of realtors and one or more neighborhoods, you're ready to take a serious look at houses. It's likely
by now you've seen some houses and want to go back for a
closer inspection.

Unless you've practically memorized your particular wants,
go back to Checklist 1c. You may even find that your search so
far means that you want to make some changes in it. Once
you're satisfied that you know what you really want, however,
don't stray *too* far from your original needs and wants.

One real estate agent in Stamford, Connecticut, told us that
with first-home buyers the house often chooses the people. They
may have started out with a particular style and size in mind,
but are attracted to something entirely different. If you feel that
happening to you, it's a signal to look with extreme care before
you fall for the house's "charm."

Amy and Lew Scotton, shopping for an old house in towns
within commuting distance of Boston, found a darling home on
a lot that backed up to a wooded area. They had gone so far as
to have its antiquity verified by an architect from the Society for
the Preservation of New England Antiquity. Everything seemed
so right about the house they'd dreamed of that they put money
down on the house and signed a contract of sale.

All was well until Amy was driving her mother out to see the
house and approached it from a different route than the lovely
old road on which the real estate agent had been escorting them.
The sad discovery: a not-at-all-desirable development of stores,
bowling alley, and restaurants was going on a stone's throw
away. Neither the realtor nor the owner would admit any mis-
representation, and a few thousand dollars and agonizing weeks
later, the Scottons went house hunting again. Meanwhile, they
took an off-season rental on Cape Cod "to take the pressure
off."

There are two good rules for looking at any house. First, get around and look at the area (a good minimum would be a five-mile radius), taking a different route every time. Second, take the pressure off. Get rid of the feeling that you won't be able to get a house if you don't do it quickly. This is certain to ensure you more time to look around so you can be selective and resistant to impulse buying.

On your first trips out, you should be making some notes about the homes you see. Record your observations of the interior and exterior and your first impressions of the house. It's also useful to take along a good pocket flashlight and a camera with instant-developing film. When you find the home or homes you really want to consider, you'll want a much more detailed evaluation, but making notes on each house that even tempts you is worth doing at this point.

Judging the Outside of a House

The exterior of the house is the first thing you, your guests, and your neighbors will see, and some of the problems or the assets of a house can best be spotted from the outside. Record your first impression: do you like the house?

Note the size, shape, and condition of the lot. Are the yards, front, side, and back, about what you will need for your family activities? Is the property well landscaped? Is the lawn in good condition? Are there any eyesores that need to be removed? Do the trees and shrubs appear healthy? Does the lot appear to be well drained?

Is there room for a garden if you want one? Has anyone in the vicinity got a garden, and is the soil suitable for gardening? Is it sizeable enough for your needs? Are there hose connections to take care of lawn and gardening needs?

Is there a garage? Is the driveway big enough to turn around in so you don't have to back out onto a busy street? If there's no driveway, what are the parking alternatives? Is the driveway steep? Will it be a problem in snowy weather?

How much privacy do you have from neighbors? Are there overhead wires or other intrusions that make your view unpleasant? How about garbage cans—are they easily hidden from view?

Does the house rely on a septic tank or a well? Are they in good condition?

Look carefully at the exterior of the house. Is the siding in good condition? Blistered paint may mean that the house is long overdue for a new paint job, but it could also mean that there's moisture in the walls.

Check the condition of the masonry in the foundation, and the chimneys. Serious cracks or missing bricks suggest you'll need to do more investigating. A sound foundation is vital. If it is not in good condition you may want to look at another house. Anything you love enough is fixable. But foundations are the most difficult and expensive—maybe even impossible and exorbitant —to fix. If you find that plastic or metal sheathing has been added to a house, ask what it was put over and note that that too will need further investigation.

Of what material and in what condition is the roof? If shingles are of wood, are they chemically fireproofed? If the roof is in poor condition, it must be repaired immediately to protect the house. This is the second most important structural detail of a house. It's a lot more fixable than a foundation, but is costly and must be done at once.

Are the gutters and leaders in good condition?

Are there storm windows and doors and/or screens in good condition? Is there weather stripping?

Are all the outside steps and porches or terraces in good condition?

How do you like the entrances? Is there a convenient entry to the kitchen for groceries? Is there a "mud" room, no matter how small? Is there an entryway or foyer or center hall at the front door to provide some degree of privacy?

The Inside of the House

As you walk through the house, imagine that you're *living* there. Does the space fit your desires? Is the kitchen at least workable, if not ideal? Do any major appliances come with it? Is there adequate laundry space?

Think about "traffic patterns." Will children have to go through the family living room to get to their bedrooms? Will you have to walk across a carpeted room to get wood from the wood box to the fireplace? Is the only egress to the backyard through the kitchen?

How soundproof is the house? Are bedrooms located far enough away from the normal activities to provide privacy? Some experts suggest adding a transistor radio to your house-testing equipment so you can check how noise travels from one area to another. It's a fair test in a furnished house, but not in a house that is empty, since noise will reverberate.

Look intently at the basics the first time around. Storage is important to comfortable living. Does each bedroom have an adequate closet? Are there separate linen and coat closets? Is there enough storage space for bicycles, trunks, boxes, luggage, off-season clothes? How is the kitchen storage space?

Check the condition of the walls. Is the plaster free from cracks and stains? Cracks can indicate some foundation problem or excessive settling of the house. Stains indicate damp side-walls or a leaking roof.

What is the condition of the floors? Are they level? One of the tricks of checking for level floors is to put a marble or small ball in the center of an uncarpeted floor. Note how fast and in what direction it rolls. Excessive speed of the roll and the same direction in every room may mean the house has settled excessively to one side and the foundation needs further investigation.

Some experts say a good indication of the condition of a house and the care it's had is to check the little things: the tub caulking; if windows open and close easily; if there are enough electrical outlets in the kitchen to serve modern housekeeping needs; if doors close with no uneven gaps.

You can check water pressure by turning on the sink and bathtub faucets and then flushing the toilet.

Walk around the rooms and look out the windows. See what your views are and note how the house is sited. Will the room or space where you breakfast be sunny or dark? Will the backyard or patio be blazing hot on a summer afternoon? Will a northern exposure of the house be an indicator of higher heating-fuel bills?

You should determine, to the extent that you can on your first trip, these five important aspects of the house you're looking at:

1. That the roof doesn't leak.
2. That the lot has proper drainage and the basement will stay dry after heavy rains.
3. That the foundation is sound and there is no indication of termite damage.
4. That the sewage disposal system is adequate and in good working order.
5. That the water supply, if private, is safe.

Judging an Old House

An old, or used or resale house offers an opportunity to ask different questions and make some wholly different observations than you would about a new house.

Though it is possible that neither a seller nor his realtor will tell you about the problems of the house, there are factual questions you can get answers to. You can find out how long the present owner has been in the house, how much he paid (the recorded deed at the town hall or county courthouse will verify that), and why he wants to sell. You can also ask to see his recent property tax and utility bills. Most of this information is a matter of public record.

If you're purchasing a house built in the last five or ten years, you may be able to talk with people who used the same builder, especially if the home is in a builder's development. While every house will have slightly different quirks, you can determine if nine out of ten people had trouble with, for example, the heating system.

If you're looking at a much older house, neighbors or townspeople may know something about the history of the house and its occupants.

Several of our interviewees declared that if the house is sound, you should ignore the decor if it's old. The surface aesthetics might not please you, but paint and paper are the easiest and cheapest—and sometimes most attractive—things you do to a house.

In an older house, it's important to check the heating (and/or cooling) system and the wiring and electricity.

The heating system may have been designed to heat the original house and may be ineffectual or inefficient in rooms that have been added on. Check carefully to know what kind of heating system exists and whether it is really in tune with energy availability. Check also to see if the insulation is adequate for the house and the climate.

Wiring and electricity in an old home may be inadequate and even dangerous. Cloth-covered wiring and some plastic wiring are fire hazards. It's best to have a good electrician inspect the wiring and the amount of current coming into the house. You might also find that you'll have to replace an old fuse box with circuit breakers.

A New House

New homes today are most likely to be found in a housing development or developing area, and in a neighborhood where the sizes, styles, and prices of the homes are much the same. This will often mean that the incomes and interests of the people who live there will also be similar. If you buy in a development, there is a certain amount of protection for your investment, since the very sameness of prices and maintenance of the properties will tend to ensure the resale value of your home.

New homes do have certain advantages. They may be better insulated and have more efficient heating systems than older homes. If it's important, they may have central air conditioning. A new home should cost less to maintain because of the use of such new materials as fiberglass and plastics. If the builder-developer has been aware of space and useful design, a new home is likely to have a more workable kitchen, with new appliances that offer such niceties as self-cleaning ovens and self-defrosting refrigerators, more storage space, more electrical outlets, and better-planned traffic patterns.

But, and it's a big but, a new home will only be as good as the materials and the construction standards that went into making it. Unfortunately, price is not necessarily a criterion for judging the worth of a new home. The real concern is to be sure you are buying from an honest builder who stands behind his work and has built good houses in the past.

Don't sign any papers or make any commitments to buying a new home until you have checked out the builder in the following four ways:

1. Find out how long he's been in business. You will usually be better off with a builder who has an established reputation in the field.

2. Check out the builder's reputation and past performance with the local Chamber of Commerce, the local Better Business Bureau, and, most of all, with previous customers. Ask people who have lived in homes he built how happy they've been with the basic systems of the home and its construction. Ask them whether he has been willing to rectify any shortcomings in the construction of the house.

3. Ask whether he is a member of the National Association of Home Builders.

4. Find out what kind of guarantee or warranty he gives that necessary adjustments or repairs will be made promptly at no extra cost to you. Ask what responsibility the builder assumes for his subcontractors. Will he take responsibility for faulty plumbing? If you are buying from a responsible builder, he will provide some warranty against major defects in your new house. Some states require certain warranties. Some local (city)builders' associations have set standards that member builders must follow.

A relatively new, voluntary program provides a comprehensive ten-year protection package that enables builders who meet certain qualifications to provide their new home buyers with major safeguards. It is the Home Owners Warranty Program (HOW). The HOW program is available to qualified builders at a very low rate, $2 per $1,000 value of the home. Ask your builder about this nationally available protection, or be sure he offers you similar coverage against structural defects.

Once you're satisfied that you're dealing with a reliable builder, check out the qualities of the building site. If the land has been filled in, has it settled enough to provide a good foundation and proper drainage? Are the lots large enough to allow the privacy you want? Has any landscaping been done? How many community amenities, such as sidewalks, sewage disposal, shopping areas, and schools, have been established? How will the addition of these affect your costs? Is the development completed? If not, what will it look like when it is?

If you're buying from a model house, it probably means the house you'll eventually own will not be completed, even started, as yet. This has the advantage of allowing you to select or make, within reason, some changes in the plan of the house you select. Usually, the builders will offer several basic plans that may be altered to suit your specific needs and desires. That's the advantage of buying from a model home, but there are areas to be wary of.

You'll need, again within reason, to get a guaranteed date of the completion of your house. One home buyer told us her new home was supposed to be ready in June. Through June, July, and August, she watched and waited. On Labor Day, her builder told her, "If your house isn't ready by September fifteenth, I shouldn't be in the building business." Barbara moved in on September 26, and she described the scene: "Carpenters were going out the back door as I came in the front. Just the day before, workmen were racing around like Keystone Cops, laying hardwood floors and putting tiles up on the bathroom wall." We talked with Barbara on November 7, and she said, "I'm still living in the middle of a construction site with a puddle for a backyard."

Look at the model as just that. It will be professionally furnished and decorated. Try to blot out the decor and see what the house would look like without all the trimmings. Be sure exactly what appliances, furnishings, built-ins, and lighting fixtures actually come with the house.

Remember that many new homes are built with "in" designs or accessories. Don't swing your decision on chandeliers or a sunken living room or a spiral staircase unless such accoutrements are your heart's desires. None of them may be "in" ten years from now.

Use the checklists in this section for recording your detailed observations on any homes you are *seriously* considering buying. Checklists 3c and 3f were designed to help you make judgments on *houses,* old or new. There are separate checklists later in the section for condominiums, cooperatives, and mobile homes.

Space has been provided on Checklist 3e for attachment of photographs to serve as a reminder of just what the house looks like. Pictures of the houses will also be a help if you want to talk over your possible purchases with other members of your family or anyone else who may be helping you make a choice.

This evaluation of houses assumes you have already checked the neighborhood and are satisfied with it. If, at this point, you happen to be directed to a house in a neighborhood that's new to you, go back to Checklist 3c, and do a thorough check on the neighborhood if the house you're seeing looks good to you. Remember the old saw about the three most important items of house judgment: location, location, and location.

How to Judge a Condominium

While condominiums and cooperatives both offer a portion of a multifamily dwelling and do represent, to different degrees, ownership of your living quarters, there are distinct differences in the way you should judge the purchase of them, particularly as regards your rights, privileges, and anticipated costs.

The search for a condominium should begin much the same as the search for a house, for condominiums come in many forms.

Originally, condominiums were built in resort areas as second or vacation homes. Now, as land costs have increased and the demand for housing is great, condominiums are the most rapidly expanding category of housing. You will find them in towering inner-city structures, in the outskirts of cities in well-planned semisuburban communities, and in suburban-country environments, often built as well-designed town houses with a wealth of community property and activities available.

Checklist 3c is just as important when you're condominium hunting as when you're house hunting. Looking at the space and the condition of the building, the grounds, and the rooms you will be sole occupant of should be subject to the same judgments applied to a house.

Just as you would take care to check the history of an old house, take particular care to check older rental buildings that have been fancied up with wall-to-wall carpeting and modern kitchen appliances and converted into condominiums. Because condominium ownership appeals to many people who want no yard to mow, no driveways to shovel, and no leaking roof to repair, it is a popular housing trend—and there are many opportunists among developers who follow trends. Don't hesitate to ask questions. If you're considering buying in a new structure, check the builder's reputation. If you are considering an older structure, check the turnover and talk with people who live there. Above all, know exactly what you will own, what the monthly maintenance will be, and whether further assessments are likely.

If you are considering a condominium purchase, you will find the following publications useful. *Questions about Condominiums,* HUD-365-F(3), June 1976, is free on request to the U.S. Department of Housing and Urban Development, Washington, DC 20410. For the *Condominium Buyer's Guide,''* send $1.00 to The National Association of Home Builders, 15th and M Streets, NW, Washington, DC 20005.

Checklists 3g and 3h provide charts for evaluating a condominium. Checklist 3i is a list of questions to ask *before* you agree to buy.

Checklist 3e. JUDGING HOUSES (OLD AND NEW)

	House #1	House #2	House #3	House #4
Location				
Style				
Total square feet				
Owner or builder Address Phone number				
Realtor Address Phone number				
Price asked				
Down payment required (if available now)				
Terms of mortgage				
Estimated monthly mortgage payments				
Estimated closing costs				
Yearly property taxes				
Estimated cost of immediate repair				

[Paste in pictures below]

(HOUSE # 1)

(HOUSE # 2)

(HOUSE # 3)

(HOUSE # 4)

Checklist 3f. RATING OLD AND NEW HOUSES

Rate each aspect of each house on a scale of 1 to 5.
1 = excellent; 2 = good; 3 = fair; 4 = I'm not sure or I think there may be a problem; 5 = there *is* a problem.

	House #1	House #2	House #3	House #4
Exterior				
The quality of the area (3–5 mile radius)				
Size of yard (according to your needs) Front				
Back				
Landscaping (if new house, this may mean check what builder provides)				
Condition of present trees and shrubs				
Condition of lawn				
Drainage of lot				
Garage				
Driveway (consider bad-weather conditions)				
Privacy from neighbors				
Freedom from traffic noise				
The view (any overhead wires or other intrusions)				
Gardening possibilities				
Patio (if any)				
Terrace (if any)				
Septic tank (if any)				
Well (if any)				
Siding (judge condition)				

	House #1	House #2	House #3	House #4
Foundation (check for any signs of termites or cracks)				
Chimneys and masonry				
Roof				
Gutters and leaders				
Porch and/or steps				
Windows and doors				
Storm windows				
Screens				
Weather-stripping				
Front entry (judge for convenience and privacy)				
Rear entrance (judge for easy access from driveway)				

Interior
Traffic patterns

Inside the house				
From inside to outside				
Space (judged against needs)				
Soundproofness				
Storage space				
Closet space				
At entrances				
In bedrooms				

	House #1	House #2	House #3	House #4
Bathrooms (check condition and number)				
Kitchen (add here any appliances that come with house. If used, check working condition)				
Sufficient electrical outlets				
Condition of walls				
Condition of floors				
Heating system				
Hot water system				
Water pressure				
Wiring				
Windows and doors (do they move freely, close tightly)				
How is the light in: Kitchen				
Living room				
Breakfast area				
Basement condition				
Fireplaces (if any)				
Insulation (if information available now)				

Notes:

Judging a Cooperative

Considering the selection of a cooperative apartment may not seem, on the surface, much more complicated than choosing a rental apartment. It *is* more complicated, however, and you should be infinitely more concerned with the condition of an apartment you buy than one you rent. Even though you don't actually own the building you live in when you buy shares in cooperative housing, you are responsible for its maintenance and repair. As a member of a nonprofit cooperative, you are expected to help set the standards for the entire building. By the same token, the neighbors you choose help set the standards, too. When buying into a cooperative venture, it is not only important to locate the right neighborhood (Checklist 3c), but to be sure you're also locating the right neighbors within the housing structure itself.

If you are considering buying into a cooperative, check out the builder carefully and be sure he is financially responsible. Have other apartments been sold to financially responsible people? When you buy into a cooperative you are really getting into co-ownership with the other shareholders. If other shareholders default on their payments, the remaining occupants will have to absorb the loss.

Ask always, perhaps first, when you're considering a cooperative purchase, what kind of mortgage you can get. You may be able to borrow 80 percent of the appraised shares representing your unit, leaving a 20 percent down payment. But the available mortgage may be as little as 50 percent or less. Check the maximum term (length) of the mortgage allowed and the interest rate. The term may be short and the interest rate high.

Check carefully to see if the price of the shares is fair, a bargain, or highly inflated. One of the measurements you can use is to add up your expected montly costs: the maintenance charges, which will probably include property taxes, and your mortgage payments. Adjust these by figuring what your tax deductions (mortgage interest and property taxes) will be. Subtract your tax deductions from your monthly outgo, and you should

Checklist 3g. JUDGING CONDOMINIUMS

	Condominium #1	Condominium #2	Condominium #3
Location			
Total square feet of unit I like			
Name of owner/builder			
Address			
Phone number			
Realtor (if any)			
Address			
Phone number			
Price of unit			
Monthly maintenance			

	Condominium #1	Condominium #2	Condominium #3
Rate of rising cost of maintenance (how much has it gone up in the last 5 years?)			
If available now:			
Mortgage down payment required			
Terms of mortgage			
Monthly mortgage payments			
Yearly property taxes, if not included in mortgage			
Usual monthly utility bills			
Estimated cost of any immediate repairs or major refurbishing			

Checklist 3h. **RATING CONDOMINIUMS**

Rate the condominiums you are seriously interested in buying on a scale of 1 to 5. 1 = excellent; 2 = good; 3 = fair; 4 = there may be a problem; 5 = there is a problem.

	Condominium:		
	#1	#2	#3

Exterior

Quality of the area

Layout and appearance of the
   development

Landscaping

Parking facilities

Privacy of the unit layout

Condition of the building/buildings

Quality of the community recreational
   facilities

(This list assumes you have used Checklist 3c to determine such amenities as schools, shopping, water supplies, transportation, sewage and garbage disposal.)

Interior

How does the space suit your needs?

Does layout provide privacy for
   family members?

Closet space

Bathrooms

Kitchen

Storage space

Adequate outlets

	Condominium:		
	#1	#2	#3
If any appliances are provided, list them here and rate their condition	_____		
Condition of walls	_____		
Condition of floors	_____		
How is soundproofing between units?	_____		
Bedroom closets	_____		
Bathroom condition	_____		
Water pressure	_____		
Adequate linen and other storage space	_____		
Working condition of windows and doors	_____		
Condition and performance of heating system	_____		
Laundry facilities	_____		
Exposure			
Is light adequate?	_____		
How's the view?	_____		

Checklist 3i. SOME QUESTIONS TO ASK BEFORE YOU CONSIDER BUYING A CONDOMINIUM

	Condominium:		
	#1	#2	#3
	Yes/No	Yes/No	Yes/No
Does the builder have a good reputation?			
Does the builder guarantee his work?			
If recreation facilities are not finished, is there a time guarantee on their completion?			
Is there a managing agent?			
Can co-owners terminate contract within a reasonable length of time?			
Can you keep a pet?			
Can you rent your unit if you wish?			
Can you sell your unit without complicated procedures?			
Will your deposit funds go into a separate escrow account?			
Will the developer provide you with a bank statement related to the account?			
Do local assessors and your developer agree on the amount of your real estate taxes?			
Is the common area assessment adequate to cover promised services?			
Are all services such as parking and recreational facilities included in your monthly assessment?			

(If the answer to all of these questions is not "Yes," find out why not and do some more shopping around.)

Notes:

be paying about what it would cost you to rent a comparable apartment.

Maintenance fees can often be the financial burden that gets out of hand, especially if you have joined a cooperative venture in an old building. The purchase price may be pleasingly low, but the costs to repair and maintain older buildings can escalate the maintenance. Be sure the cooperative management has provided enough working capital in the purchase price to make any major repairs and necessary updating of wiring and plumbing. You can't just be interested in the unit you will occupy. If the building roof leaks or the elevator needs to be replaced, it's all part of your financial responsibility as a shareholder.

Use checklists 3j, 3k, and 3l to make comparisons between cooperatives you're seriously interested in buying.

Judging a Manufactured Home

There are three possible ways to acquire a manufactured (panelized or precut) home. First, you may buy one through a developer or builder and you may or may not know that his homes are all built with panels that have been constructed in a factory. In this case, you'll judge the house as you would judge any new or used house. However, you may choose to build a manufactured home yourself on your own land or have a local builder do all or part of the work for you. If you decide on either of these plans, you have some special judgments and decisions to make.

Your first job is a little like collecting travel folders and dreaming about your next vacation: you should start collecting catalogues of manufacturers of precut or panelized homes. You will find a good selection of these manufacturers in the *Guide to Manufactured Homes* in the List of Booklets at the back of this book. These firms will be members of the National Association of Home Manufacturers and, frequently, members of the National Association of Home Builders; both affiliations are indications of a dedication to the principles of the associations. They will have been in business for an established length of time and their homes will represent proven architectural design. From the

Checklist 3j. JUDGING COOPERATIVES

	Co-op #1	Co-op #2	Co-op #3
Location			
Total square feet in unit I like			
Name of owner and/or builder			
Address			
Phone number			
Realtor (if any)			
Address			
Phone number			
Asking price of unit			
Current monthly maintenance			
Has monthly maintenance held the line of reasonable increase? (rise in last 5 years?)			

	Co-op #1	Co-op #2	Co-op #3
Mortgage down payment required			
Terms of mortgage			
Monthly mortgage payments			
Usual monthly utility bills			
Estimated cost of immediate repairs or redecorating			

135

Checklist 3k. RATING CO-OPS

Rate the cooperatives you are seriously interested in buying on a scale of 1 to 5. 1 = excellent; 2 = good; 3 = fair; 4 = there may be a problem; 5 = there is a problem.

	Cooperative:		
	#1	#2	#3

Exterior

Appearance of the building or complex ⸻

Landscaping (if any) ⸻

Parking facilities ⸻

Condition of the building: is it neat and well cared for? ⸻

Appearance of the surrounding buildings ⸻

(This list assumes you have used Checklist 3c).

Interior

Condition of interior hallways ⸻

Is elevator service good? ⸻

If no elevators, do stairs have adequate railings and safeguards? ⸻

How does the unit available suit your needs? ⸻

What is the overall condition of the unit? ⸻

Does layout provide privacy for family members? ⸻

Storage space ⸻

Closet space ⸻

Basement storage: is it safe and adequate? ⸻

	Cooperative:		
	#1	#2	#3
Bathrooms			
Water pressure			

Kitchen
    Storage space arrangement: is it
    workable?			

Appliances (list any appliances that come with the kitchen and rate their condition)			
Are electrical outlets adequate?			
Condition of walls			
Condition of floors			
How is soundproofing between units?			
Bedroom closets			
Condition and performance of heating system			
Laundry facilities			

Exposure
    Is light adequate?
    Are views pleasing?			

Checklist 3I. SOME QUESTIONS TO ASK BEFORE YOU CONSIDER BUYING A CO-OP

	Cooperative:		
	#1	#2	#3
	Yes/No	Yes/No	Yes/No

If new:

Have other units been sold to financially responsible people?

Does builder/developer have a sound background? Is he financially responsible?

Is the asking price fair?

If old:

What has been the turnover rate of the units? (if large, try to find out why)

Has the maintenance had a steady but reasonable rate of increase?

Are the guidelines that dictate your rights to resell clear and equitable?

Has the cooperative been a happy, problem-free venture? (ask the people who live there)

If the answer to all of these questions is not "Yes," find out why not or do some more shopping around.

NOTES:

available designs you can choose a columned colonial, a compact ranch-style, a Cape Cod, or even an "antique" that has old timbers and beams incorporated into its manufacture. Once you've made some choices, ask the manufacturer to supply you with the names of some of his customers in your area. Then talk to them and get evaluations and perhaps some good advice about the homes and anything they would have done differently.

One word of warning: there are innumerable options in manufactured homes just as there may be in any other home that is being built for you. Basic among your options is a variety of floor plans which may or may not alter the basic price. The known price of the completed house is one of the advantages of the manufactured house, but if you select too many extra items you can quickly run up the cost of the home. For example, double-pane windows may be well worth the extra cost in terms of energy saving, but a redwood deck on the back of the house may be something you can live without for the first few years. It can always be added later. If a given brand of kitchen appliances comes with the house, remember that they have been bought from a manufacturer in quantity at a quantity price. If you want another brand substituted, you will pay dearly for it. It would be better to make that change locally when the old appliance needs replacement.

To whatever extent you may use a local builder, be sure he is an established builder and has done satisfactory work in the area. Ask if he is a member of the National Association of Home Builders. Talk with people for whom he's worked. Be sure that he stands behind his work and will give you a satisfactory warranty. If you plan to do some of the work yourself, get a firm commitment on the cost of the work you plan to purchase. Checklist 3m will help you in planning and purchasing a manufactured precut or panelized home.

Judging a Mobile Home

There are three very different ways to acquire a mobile home, and they take different kinds of evaluation and require some

Checklist 3m. PLANNING THE PURCHASE OF A MANUFACTURED HOME

	Home #1	Home #2	Home #3
Name of manufacturer			
Address of manufacturer			
Style of home			
Floor plan selected			
Size of home in square feet			
Base price of home (without land)			
Price of land (if not already owned)			
Price of extras:			
Cost of construction (list all work you plan to purchase)			
Grading of land			
Laying foundation			

	Home #1	Home #2	Home #3
Erection of home			
Interior finishing			
Landscaping (including laying of sidewalks and entry walks)			
Tie-in to water supply			
Tie-in to sewage disposal			
Utility installations			
Other necessary costs			
Estimated Total Cost of Home:			

Checklist 3n. JUDGING A NEW MOBILE HOME

	#1	#2	#3
Location (unless you're putting home on your own land)			
Name of retailer/developer Address Phone number			
Purchase price of home			
Down payment required			
Terms of mortgage			
Estimated monthly mortgage cost (including taxes)			
Is 1-year warranty provided (yes or no)			
List furnishings that come with purchase price (usually kitchen range, refrigerator, water heater, furnace, furniture, draperies, carpeting, lamps)			

	#1	#2	#3

List desired extras and enter their
quoted prices (such as air
conditioning, dishwasher, laundry
equipment, storm windows and/or
screens, shutters, awning,
carport)

Does purchase price include:
Setting up and leveling home?
Installation of skirting around
the bottom?

Does house bear UL safety seal
of approval (a key to safe wiring)?

How soon can you expect delivery?

Checklist 3o. JUDGING A MOBILE HOME IN A RENTAL PARK

	#1	#2	#3
Location			
Name of park manager			
Telephone number			
Purchase price of home			
Down payment required			
Estimated monthly mortgage cost (including taxes)			
Monthly lot rental			
Extra costs for utilities, surcharges for pets, children, other (list with actual costs)			
Do the recreational facilities suit you?			
Does the ambience of the community suit you?			

	#1	#2	#3
Is the community physically attractive?			
Does the home bear the UL seal of approval?			
List appliances or furnishings that come with the purchase price of the home			
List desired extra furnishings and their estimated cost			
Are parking spaces and regulations to your liking?			
Are pets allowed?			

(The judgment questions above assume you have checked out the neighborhood (Checklists 3c, 3d) to determine the availability of schools, shopping facilities, churches and available public transportation.)

145

different questions to be asked before you decide to purchase. (1) You may own your own land and plan to site a mobile home on it. (2) You may be purchasing an existing mobile home or a new one to site in a rental park (you rent the land). (3) You may be purchasing a mobile home *and* land in a development.

In all instances, go about checking out the integrity and the past performance of the retailer, the park management, or the developer just as carefully as you would check out a builder. Ask a retailer to supply you with names and addresses of customers. Talk with them and ask how they have liked their homes and if the retailer has made good any defects. Talk with people who live in a rental park. You can quickly find out whether they are happy with the management and the community. If you're considering a development community, check the Better Business Bureau, the local Chamber of Commerce, and local banks to determine whether the developer has a sound financial reputation. Talk with people who have bought and lived in the community. Especially if the development is new, check carefully to see what neighborhood amenities are there or planned.

Whether you're considering a small (single-wide) basic model or a more luxurious model (double-wide) with such added niceties as a fireplace, a second bathroom, a front porch, and a two-car garage, be sure you know exactly what is included in the purchase price of the house and what will be considered extras.

If you plan to purchase a basic model and gradually add on extras, be sure the size of the lot and the zoning laws, or rules of the park or development, allow for planned expansion.

When you site a mobile home on your own land, you choose your community and your neighbors, but when you move into a park or development community, you are joining an existing group of people. Check carefully; knock on doors if necessary. Find out whether the community is largely young people with children, primarily an adult community, or some combination of these. Check to see what recreational facilities are available. Mobile home parks and developments tend to have a strong community spirit and, depending upon the size of the lots, a limited degree of privacy. Shop carefully to be sure your personal needs and interests will be served.

If you are buying a resale home, check all the fixtures, condition of walls, floors, and appliances just as you would in any home you plan to purchase. Check the heating system, the hot-water heater capacity. Talk, if you can, with the previous occupants to see if they have any particular complaints about the home. Check carefully the condition of the home. Also check available exits in case of fire. New mobile homes are much improved in safety and design. Older ones should be examined with care.

Traditionally, the resale value of mobile homes does not tend to rise much, especially when compared with the more traditional house. But Sherry and Bob Eberhardt, back in Chapter 2, did manage to turn a profit, and things are changing.

Use checklists 3n and 3o to judge any mobile home you consider purchasing. On questions that call for "yes or no" answers, "yes" is preferred.

MORE HELP WANTED

At this point, you should have zeroed in on *the house* and you'll need to get several next steps organized at one time: (1) getting a lawyer, (2) hiring an appraiser/building inspector, and (3) searching for your money (that's the next chapter). Don't, repeat *don't,* sign anything, formal or informal, until you've accomplished these steps.

Finding a good lawyer and a good appraiser is important to you. Your realtor may have suggestions. Ask always for the names of other clients they've served and check to see if they have been satisfied with the services they received. You might also check the local banks which extend mortgages. They have need to use appraisers/inspectors whose work they trust.

No matter what kind of housing you're buying, there will be, along the line, several binding documents to be signed. While there have been attempts made to put sale contracts into plain language, you have enough other decisions and responsibilities at this point to be bothered with the fine print and fine points of a contract of sale, a title search, or a deed. Leave it to a lawyer in the area where you plan to buy; he will be licensed to practice in that state. Choose one who is knowledgeable about real estate dealings. You may be urged to use the lawyer provided by the seller. Don't! The seller's lawyer represents one set of interests. You want someone working for your interests all along the way. Engage him now so you'll be ready when you reach the point of signing an agreement to buy.

Simultaneously, hire an appraiser or housing inspector to go over the house (or the condominium/cooperative structure) with you before you make a firm decision to buy. While you're going over the house with an appraiser, begin to fill in the final evaluation sheets of Checklist 3p. They will not only serve as a detailed check on the condition of every part of the house, but will also be invaluable as organization records when you move. What you and the appraiser/inspector find on close examination of the house may well give you some bargaining clout on the price of the house, perhaps enabling you to save enough to pay the inspection fee and then some.

When you and your appraiser/inspector have completed your final checks, you may have found some necessary repairs are needed. Get an estimate on what these will cost to do. If necessary, call in an electrician or a plumber or a roofing expert—whatever is needed—to give you a fair idea of costs. If you find serious problems with the condition of the house and still wish to buy it, you should be able to make some adjustment on the purchase price with the inspector's report and the estimates for repair in hand.

The Lawyer's First Job

If, by now, you have come to an agreed-upon price with the seller, the next step is to formalize a commitment for you to buy the house and for the seller to agree to sell it to you. This, like all other transactions in real estate, goes by a variety of names, depending upon the language used in the locality. (See the Home Buyer's Dictionary in the back of the book: you will find it useful as you wade on into the mechanics of buying the house.) The formal agreement you make at this time may be called contract of purchase, a contract for sale, an offer to buy, a binder, a memo, or a purchase agreement. When it is executed you will probably be expected to make a deposit of "good faith," which is often called "earnest money." If all the conditions of the agreement are met, the "earnest money" is earnest, indeed. You can't get it back just by changing your mind! While the language and the individual stipulations of a contract to purchase will differ in each individual transaction, this is what you and your lawyer will want in it:

- The agreed-upon purchase price.
- When and how the money is to be paid. (If you are planning to borrow money to meet the purchase price, there should be a clause in the contract that says you will be released from the agreement—and get your earnest money back —if you can't get a mortgage or a loan.)
- A description of the property, including the dimensions of the lot.
- An itemization of what portion of property taxes, insurance, water or fuel charges, due in the year of purchase, you will be expected to pay.
- A guarantee that the seller will provide you with a clear title to the property and a specified deed at the time of closing.
- A guarantee that you will get back your deposit if the deal falls through for any reason other than your failure to meet your part of the agreement.
- Any other agreement reached between you and the seller (such as the seller's commitment to remove trash from the yard, have a termite exterminator in, or remove a dead tree from the property). Any verbal promises should be put in writing now.
- The seller's signature making the agreement binding.

Rely on your lawyer for any special legalities pertaining to your transaction, but insist upon understanding what every clause means. Your lawyer is not only your protector, he's your interpreter.

Checklist 3p. FINAL CHECKLIST FOR THE HOUSE

Items starred are ones you want to be sure are covered by your appraiser/inspector)

Notes and Observations

Exterior

- What type of soil is the home built on?

- Is the lot properly drained?

- Is there any evidence of settling that would damage the foundation or the walls of the house?

- Are the foundation walls in good condition?

- Does the house meet local zoning laws?

- What is the condition of the sewage system?

- What is the condition of the exterior walls?

- What is the condition of the roof?
  - Will it need any repairs?
  - If wood-shingled, are they fireproofed?

- Are gutters and leaders in good condition?

- Are storm windows and/or screens in good condition?

- Is the masonry in good condition? (includes chimneys, fireplaces, walkways, foundation, basement floor)

- Are door and window locks adequate?

- Are there any special security measures needed?

- Is there any indication of termite damage?

- Does the house have a northern exposure that suggests heating bills may be high?

- Is the garage in good condition? Is it adequate for your

- Is it adequate for your needs? (Can you use present wiring for air conditioning, and electric stove, etc., without shorting all the fuses or starting a fire?)
  - Are there sufficient electrical outlets?
- What is the condition of the plumbing?
- Is the drinking water pure?
- Do all the faucets and drainpipes work well?
- Is the water pressure adequate?
- What is the condition of the heating system?
- What is the condition of the hot-water heating system?
  - Is it adequate for your needs?
- Is the basement in good condition?
  - Is it dry?
  - Is it well ventilated?
- What is the condition of the attic?
- Is the house adequately insulated?
- Are the floors in good condition?
  - If carpeted, what's underneath?
- Are the walls in good condition?
- Are steps and stairs in good condition?
- Are moldings and baseboards in good condition?
- If there's a fireplace, does it work properly?
- Do windows and doors fit properly?
- If there's central air conditioning, does it work properly?

151

Notes and Observations

- If any major appliances or other machinery (such as power lawn mower) come with the house, do they work properly? List each and note the condition *after* you've tested them out.

Kitchen:

- Overall dimensions (if you feel it would be helpful, use ¼-inch graph paper and record layout of kitchen to show placement and dimensions of cabinets and appliances)

- Amount of counter space and work surfaces

- Amount of shelf and cabinet storage space

- Condition of kitchen floor
  - Will it be easy to clean?

- Is there room for an eating area in the kitchen?

- Is kitchen adjacent to dining room or other eating areas?

- What is the condition of the kitchen walls?
  - Are they easy to keep clean?

- Will you have to do any major refurbishing to make the kitchen workable or suitable to your needs? If so, enter estimated cost of changes. (include any major appliances such as stove or refrigerator)

Bathrooms:

- Are electrical outlets adequate for personal appliance needs?

Notes and Observations

• Is grout in tiled areas in good condition?
  • If not, is there any indication of moisture in interior walls?

Bedrooms:

• Overall dimensions (use graph paper to show room dimensions, locations of any irregular walls or built-ins)

• Condition of floors

• Type of floor covering needed

• Is there an adequate closet?

• Is there adequate ventilation?

Living Room:

• Overall dimensions (use graph paper to show room dimensions, locations of any irregular walls or built-ins)

• Condition of floors
  • Will they need new carpeting?
  • Will they need refinishing?

• Condition of walls
  • Do they need paint?
  • Are they in condition to take wall covering?

• Is there good ventilation?

• Is there pleasing light?

153

The next step you should ask your lawyer to initiate is a *title search*. A title represents your right to the ownership of a piece of property. It represents your right to use the property (according to zoning regulations), and your right to sell it later if you wish. A title search will reveal whether there are any liens or encumbrances due to unpaid taxes or mortgages that would prevent the seller from giving you a clear title to the property you wish to purchase. In many instances the title insurance company you use will perform this service. While your lawyer is pursuing the title search, it's time for you to commence the search for your money to complete the purchase of your chosen home.

4

The Search for the Money

HELP WANTED

If you have enough money to put down for the full payment on
a house you want to buy, you can skip this chapter. But if you're
in the housing market for the first time, it's likely you'll need a
mortgage to finance the purchase of a home. If "search" seems
like a strong word to use for the step of finding mortgage money,
believe that it isn't. Search implies that you're going to look at
all possibilities and weigh them carefully, and that kind of looking can save you money.

Here again, it will pay you to talk to everyone you can about
the ways, the means, and the places where you can find mortgage money and at what price. Talk to friends who have been
through it. Talk to acquaintances you've made as you've been
house hunting. Find out what they found out about any special
helps for first-time home buyers. Some states have provided
subsidies for young, first-time buyers. Some communities have
monies available to help if you plan to go into an area slated for

renovation. Visit your town, city, or county Housing Administration offices. Ask about any places they know of. Making money available for young-family housing has been a concern of many cities, towns, and counties. Check carefully so you don't miss anything.

The housing market and the concern, especially government's concern, for helping people achieve adequate housing has been a continually changing one. Be sure you find out all you can about possible help and direction. Shopping for the right mortgage is just as important as shopping for the right neighborhood or the right house.

There are established institutions that will help, directly and indirectly, in your search. See them, solicit their help, and ask, ask, ask about anything you don't understand or anything you want to know about the mortgage market.

Your own bank is a good place to start. If it is a full-service commercial bank or a savings bank, it probably handles mortgage loans. Even if it isn't a mortgage-writing bank, talk to one of the officers there, preferably one who has some knowledge of real estate transactions. He should have your interests at heart; after all, they have your money in their bank. He will be able to give you advice and guidance about current interest rates, the advisability of your considering an FHA-insured loan, your eligibility for a VA loan (coming up later in this section). He can certainly tell you about the mortgage-lending policies of his own bank. Make notes as you talk. When you go over your notes later, you may have more questions. You can always go back and ask them another time.

If your bank does deal in mortgages, ask these five essential questions in relationship to the funds you have on hand, your monthly housing estimates, and the house you have in mind:

1. What is the current mortgage interest rate?
2. How much down payment is required?
3. What length of repayment period would he suggest for a mortgage?
4. How much would he estimate the closing costs to be?

5. Would he anticipate any "points" being charged in this transaction? (A point is 1 percent of the mortgage, and you'll be hearing more about this shortly.)

How does his evaluation fit your monthly ability to pay? There are a myriad of details to be discussed and the bank will want to make an evaluation of the house before any firm commitment is made. You are simply asking first things first.

If you are moving to another state, you will need to talk to a local banker there about mortgages, preferably at a bank you intend to use for your other banking needs. Banks don't like crossing state lines when it comes to mortgages.

FHA (Federal Housing Administration) loans, as they're often referred to, are not really loans but mortgage insurance programs. FHA is a division of the Department of Housing and Urban Development (HUD), and is authorized to administer that department's housing-assistance program. FHA financing protects the mortgage lender from financial loss. It doesn't protect the borrower, but it does allow him to get a loan with a lower down payment, lower interest rates, and a longer mortgage term (repayment period), because the federal government insures the repayment of the loan. Finance terms vary with the programs, and from time to time changes are made in the regulations. Limitations and interest rates are also adjusted periodically to reflect market conditions.

The two programs most associated with single-family financing are *Home Mortgage Insurance* (HUD Section 203[b]) and the *Graduated Payment Mortgage Program* (HUD Section 245). In 1979, the maximum insurable mortgage under the Home Mortgage Insurance program was $60,000. See your regional HUD-FHA office to inquire about all of their programs and how you may qualify for assistance under them. Or write to the Federal Housing Administration, Department of Housing and Urban Development, 451 7th Street, NW, Washington, DC 20410.

Remember that your loan will still come from a local lending institution. Know, too, that many banks prefer not to be involved in the paperwork an FHA-insured loan requires, and that they are not often happy with the lower interest rates. They may be completely reluctant to deal with these programs, or may charge you points to offset these disadvantages to them. Nevertheless, with so many advantages available through these programs, it's worth a try.

The VA (Veterans Administration) Guaranteed Home Loan program is available to veterans, beginning with those of World War II. It is also available to unmarried surviving spouses of service personnel who died in the service or from a service-connected disability, and to the wives of servicemen who have been captured or are listed as missing in action. This program guarantees up to 60 percent or $25,000, whichever is less, of a loan made to purchase, construct, alter, improve, or repair a home, a property consisting of not more than four units, or a one-family residential unit in a condominium development approved by the VA. The VA will also guarantee a loan made to purchase a mobile home. The VA guarantee usually takes the place of a down payment to the lender, and the maximum interest rate is generally lower. Any local lending institution approved by the VA can process the loan. Here again, time and paperwork are involved that lending institutions may resist. You can go to your regional Veterans Administration office and make some inquiries about your benefits under this program, and initiate an application for your Certificate of Eligibility. That certificate does not guarantee approval of a loan, but it is a necessary first step. If you are eligible, it's worth looking into the process and benefits of a VA-insured (often called a GI) loan. If you are not near a regional VA office, write to the Veterans Administration, Washington, DC 20420

The FmHA (Farmers Home Administration), an agency of the Department of Agriculture, administers two direct loan programs to provide housing for low- and moderate-income families living in rural areas. One of them, the *FmHA Homeownership Program,* has recently been expanded to guarantee loans for middle-class home buyers. If you are planning to settle in a rural area, look into this program to see if you might qualify. FmHA offices will probably be located in the county seat. If not, a county official can direct you to the proper place for inquiry, or you can write to the Farmers Home Administration, Department of Agriculture, Washington, DC 20250.

KINDS OF MORTGAGES

Once you have checked out the possibility of some help from any of the federally sponsored housing programs, and inquired about any state or locally subsidized programs for which you may be eligible, you are ready to go shopping for your mortgage money. The places to check are numerous.

Start with a savings and loan institution, where you're likely to get the most favorable terms. Also check commercial banks, savings banks, life insurance companies, and mortgage banking companies. If you belong to a credit union, check to see if they offer mortgages. Some do. If you are buying a new home in a development, it is quite possible your builder will have arranged to have mortgage money available. Check to see what he offers.

As you shop, you will learn that there are two basic kinds of mortgages available. They are known as the conventional, or standard, fixed-payment mortgage and the graduated-payment mortgage.

The conventional, standard, fixed-payment mortgage is still the most widely used. It simply means that after the down payment, the monthly costs for the life (repayment period) of the mortgage will remain the same.

The graduated-payment mortgage (GPM) is gaining great popularity among younger families. These mortgages are now available on homes financed with FHA-insured mortgages and from any savings and loan association.

The appeal of the GPM is that it allows young families to qualify for a more expensive home than they could get with a conventional mortgage. It provides lower monthly payments in the first five years of the mortgage. The payments gradually rise until, in the sixth year, they reach a fixed rate. They then remain the same for the life of the mortgage. The interest rate remains constant, as it does in a conventional, fixed-payment mortgage. The lower monthly payments are made possible in the first five years by putting the home buyer's down payment in a pledged savings account which is drawn from each month to supplement the lower mortgage payment. Under the FHA-insured GPMs, there are five plans available. They differ in the rate of payment increase and in the length of time the increase continues. Another GPM instrument, known as FLIP (Flexible Loan Insurance Program), is used by some developer/builders. It offers customized plans for prospective buyers.

A few states offer *roll-over mortgages* (ROM) and *variable-rate mortgages* (VRM). With the roll-over mortgage, the interest rate may be adjusted every five years. Variable-rate mortgages may have their rate adjusted every six months. People have chosen these mortgages because they guarantee transferability of the mortgage, less severe prepayment penalties, line-of-credit provisions, and an initial interest rate that is ¼ percent below that of the standard, fixed-payment mortgage. Lenders like these mortgages because they give them a hedge against inflation. Under the standard, fixed-payment mortgage, the borrower gets the hedge against inflation but not the opportunity to benefit if interest rates go down.

You may also have reason to discuss an *open-end mortgage*. This may allow you to borrow more money in the future without rewriting the mortgage. It is a convenience if you want to expand your home at some future date.

Whatever you do, be sure to avoid a balloon mortgage. It carries a large last payment that can be surprisingly enormous. It might even lose you your house.

HOW TO EVALUATE MORTGAGE CONDITIONS

The most common concern of first-time home buyers is, "Can we manage the monthly costs?" This is perfectly natural. Most first-home buyers have been used to monthly rental charges, and that is the easiest financial framework in which to compute where the money's going. That, however, is really the bottom line in the whole transaction, not the first consideration that you should use in evaluating the conditions under which you select a mortgage lender.

Lending institutions will have different *down-payment requirements*. A substantial down payment can bring several advantages. Obviously, the more you put into the down payment, the lower your monthly payments will be, the more equity you will have in your home, and the less interest you'll have to pay over the life of the mortgage.

If, for example, you put a $10,000 payment down on a $40,000 home and got a twenty-five-year mortgage at 9 percent interest, your monthly payment would be $252. Over the twenty-five years, $45,530 of your payments would have gone to paying interest. If you put only $5,000 down on the same house with the same mortgage terms, your monthly payments would be $294 and the interest at the end of twenty-five years would be $53,120. As you can see, the interest you pay can far exceed the cost of the house itself, and while you have to save enough of your savings for closing costs, moving expenses, and expected emergencies, the higher your down payment, the lower your overall costs of purchasing will be. Also, it's possible a lender will offer a more liberal interest rate with a higher down payment.

The *interest rates* in any given locality are likely to be much the same, but a ½ percent to 1 percent difference is a matter of a lot of money over a period of years. During the early years of a mortgage, a very small amount of the monthly payments is applied to the principal because a large portion goes to paying the interest on the loan. The interest rate must be one of the most important shopping considerations you ask about. For example, if you took a $40,000 mortgage for a twenty-five-year-repayment period at a 9 percent interest rate, you would be paying out, in those twenty-five years, $60,700 in interest. The same loan for the same amount of time at a 9½ percent interest rate would cost you $64,840 in total interest. Raise the interest rate to 10 percent and you'll pay out roughly $69,040. That figures out to be a little over $4,000 for a ½ percent difference in interest rate, and more than $8,000 for a 1 percent difference. All other conditions being equal, you can't afford not to shop for the best interest rate you can find, knowing that even half a percentage point will amount to a considerable saving.

The length, or term or repayment period, of the mortgage you choose will also have a great effect on the amount of interest you pay. A long-term mortgage has the advantage of lower monthly payments and leaving more money to be applied to other living expenses. But if you take the long-range view, a long-term mortgage is a costly affair. Figuring the annual interest rate at 9 percent, the interest you would pay on a fifteen-year mortgage would be a little over 80 percent of the original loan. If you take as long as thirty years to pay off the mortgage, the total interest you pay is about *double* the amount of the original loan! To put the comparison in real figures, a $40,000 loan at 9 percent for fifteen years would cost you $33,030 in total interest, with monthly payments of around $406. The same loan for thirty years would cost you $75,860 in total interest, with monthly payments of $322. Obviously, the shorter the time taken to repay the loan, the lower the total cost of interest will be to you.

These three basics—amount of down payment, interest rate, and length of mortgage—are the most influential factors on the cost of your home, and the first considerations you must work out with your lender. There are, however, other questions to be asked as you shop around.

Ask about points. When money is scarce or tight and the general trend of interests rates is up, lending institutions may charge you ''points'' to make up the difference between the state-regulated interest ceilings and the yield they can get elsewhere in the money market. Also, because of the lower interest rates on FHA- and VA-insured loans, this point principal is applicable to them. One point is equal to 1 percent of the loan. Thus, if your loan were for $40,000 and the lender is charging you five points, you'd be paying a one-time charge of $2,000. Or you'd be taking out a $40,000 loan but only getting $38,000 of it. Some lenders may call this charge a ''discount'' or ''discount points.'' Be sure to put the question to every lender you interview.

Ask about prepayment penalties. The most desirable arrangement you can have on a mortgage is the privilege of prepaying your mortgage loan before maturity without any penalty. Some lenders will not allow any prepayment unless you forfeit an interest refund on the amount you prepay. Some will not allow any prepayment without penalty for a specified period of time, usually in the first year. If you accumulate some extra cash, or if your earnings increase sharply and you want to pay off your mortgage in a shorter time, you could save a lot of interest money. Shop for a lender who will allow prepayment with no or minimal penalties.

Ask about late-payment penalties. Check with lenders to find out what grace period they allow, if any, in the event you have to miss a payment. How long will they allow you to make that payment without a penalty? How big is the penalty after the grace period has elapsed? Late charges should not be more than 4 percent to 6 percent of the payment.

Ask how quickly you can expect to get the loan, assuming that it will be approved. Ask especially if you are considering applying for an FHA- or VA-insured loan.

Ask about an open-ended mortgage. If you want to, in effect, borrow more money by increasing your monthly payments or extending the life or term of the mortgage, can you do it at the same rate of interest you got on the original mortgage? Check carefully to see what extra costs may be involved.

Ask about estimated closing costs. Though property taxes, fire insurance, title insurance, appraisal fees, survey fees, and many other possible closing costs you'll learn more about in the next chapter may sound baffling to you, the lender deals with them all the time and he should be familiar enough with local practices and fees to give you a fair estimate of what you can expect. He can certainly give you a decisive answer on what the lending institution's fee is for processing the mortgage application.

Ask whether an escrow account is usual or required. It would be used to cover taxes, insurance, and some other expenses. Ask whether the lender will give you interest on the escrow money.

Ask about home insurance. How much home insurance must you carry to get the mortgage? Some lenders require that you take your insurance through them. That does not leave you free to shop for the best terms you can get on insurance, and may mean that the lender is also making a profit on the insurance he demands you carry to secure the loan. Ask if there are any other charges that you haven't asked about. You will have to be prepared to reveal all sorts of information to your lender, so you can ask, and expect, him to be completely open and honest with you. Tell him you don't like surprises. For your part, be prepared to tell your lender where you work, how long you've worked there, how much you earn, the size of your family, how much rent you've been paying, how many debts you have, any installment contracts you're paying and how much you owe on them, how much you have in the bank, how old you are, what charge accounts you have, and so on.

HOW TO SELECT A LENDER

In view of the amount of money involved, your final choice of a lender should depend on the one that offers you the very best deal financially. You will be dealing with people, and it's always easier to deal with people you like and enjoy than with someone who makes you feel uncomfortable. However, this is one time you should be as objective as possible, see as many people as possible, and keep a careful record of the facts. Try to see at least one each of the lending institutions available to you: a savings and loan association, a savings bank, one or more commercial banks, one or more life insurance companies, a mortgage company, the new-home builder if you're looking at a new home, or your credit union if you have one.

If you've found your home through a realtor who's been particularly helpful, ask him to suggest some good lending institutions. He can probably steer you to some banks that offer good mortgages. Don't overlook talking to a company official where you're employed. It's possible the bank that handles their business will give good mortgage terms to the company's employees.

There is one other type of mortgage you might happen upon. It is called a *purchase-money mortgage*. If you are buying from older owners who are moving to a smaller place or retiring, it is possible to negotiate a purchase-money mortgage directly with the seller, at an interest rate and under terms you negotiate directly with the seller. Sometimes retirees would prefer the monthly income from the sale of their house to a lump-sum payment. They may even give you a slightly better interest rate than conventional lending institutions would.

Use Checklist 4a to keep notes comparing the terms offered by each lender you see.

THE DOWN PAYMENT

If, after all your scouting around, you find that you can't come up with the down payment required, you should review your buying power carefully to see if you're aiming to buy too much house at this time. However, if everything else fits your financial planning and the down payment is the only stumbling block, you can turn to what is known in the real estate business as "magic money." One realtor we talked with said this was common practice among her first-home buyers. This money comes from insurance companies that guarantee mortgages. The biggest and best-known company in the field is the Mortgage Guarantee Insurance Corporation (MGIC). The name of that company is the reason this kind of insurance is called "magic money" regardless of which insurance company is involved.

It may seem somewhat magic because you can use the insurance to get a mortgage of between 90 percent and 95 percent of the home's appraised value. The lending institutions you've seen may want a 20 percent or 25 percent down payment. Suppose you are looking at a $50,000 home and the bank wants a 20 percent down payment, or $10,000. If you don't have $10,000 to put down, you can turn to an insurance company like MGIC to insure the difference between a 20 percent down payment ($10,000) and a 5 percent down payment ($2,500). For this insurance, you pay 1 percent of the mortgage at the closing or, in this

Checklist 4a. CONVENTIONAL MORTGAGE (STANDARD, FIXED-PAYMENT)

Name, Address, and Phone Number of Lender	Will Write FHA, VA, FmHA Mortgages	Down Payment Required	Interest Rate	Mortgage Terms (list choices available)	Points (how many?)	Prepayment Terms
#1						
#2						
#3						
#4						

Late-Payment Grace Period (grace or penalty)	Monthly Payment (does it include property taxes or insurance?)	How Long to Get Loan?	Open-Ended Mortgage (terms?)	Estimated Closing Costs	Home Insurance (can it be bought separately?)	Other Notes (such as necessary deposits)
#1						
#2						
#3						
#4						

Name, Address and Phone Number of Lender	Will Write FHA, VA, FmHA Mortgages	Down Payment Required	Interest Rate	Mortgage Terms (list choices available)	Points (how many?)	Prepayment Terms
#5						
#6						
#7						
#8						

Late-Payment Grace Period (grace or penalty)	Monthly Payment (does it include property taxes or insurance?)	How Long to Get Loan?	Open-Ended Mortgage (terms?)	Estimated Closing Costs	Home Insurance (can it be bought separately?)	Other Notes (such as necessary deposits)
#5						
#6						
#7						
#8						

GRADUATED PAYMENT MORTGAGES

Name, Address, and Phone Number of Lender	Will Lender Write FHA-Guaranteed Loan?	Down Payment Required	Monthly Payments					
			Year 1	Year 2	Year 3	Year 4	Year 5	Year 6
#1								
#2								
#3								
#4								

Terms of Mortgage	Interest Rate	Points	Estimated Closing Costs	Prepayment Terms	Late-Payment Grace Period and/or Penalty	How Long to Get Loan?	Other Notes
#1							
#2							
#3							
#4							

instance, $475. You will pay the rest of the insurance in install-
ments, usually over a ten-year period. In this example, it would
amount to a little over $100 a year. The mortgage company is
really insuring only the difference between $10,000 and $2,500
or, in this case, $7,500. But for relatively little cost you are
buying a house with a down payment you can manage, albeit
you have a bigger mortgage to pay off.

5

The Closing

Of all the observations that might be made about the necessary evil known as "closing costs," the most applicable would be that they vary greatly depending on where you live, where you get your mortgage, and how the closing is handled. It would also be fair to say that for inexperienced home buyers, they come as a painful shock, since they can run anywhere from several hundred to a few thousand dollars. In the past, the shock usually didn't come until closing day, when the buyer was expected to sit down and write check after check for fees and services he previously knew nothing about.

Now, a federal law known as the Real Estate Settlement Procedures Act (RESPA) has somewhat modified the shock by making regulations that at least give the buyer some warning. When a buyer applies for a loan, the lender must give the prospective buyer a copy of a forty-page booklet called *Settlement Costs*, prepared and approved by the Department of Housing and Urban Development (HUD). That is none too soon to get this booklet. It takes careful reading and high motivation to absorb all it has to say, some of it in very fine print. RESPA also legislates that the lender must give an applicant for a loan a "good faith'' estimate of most of the closing charges. Then, by law and at the request of the buyer, the lender is obliged to give the buyer all information relevant to closing charges *one business day* before the settlement.

HELP WANTED

Your lawyer, whom you have already lined up and who has gone over the contract of sale with you, should continue to represent your interests by reviewing any and all documents that have to do with the mortgage and the transfer of the real estate. Sometimes the buyer will be asked to pay for the seller's lawyer and the bank lawyer. Be wary of that arrangement and of the suggestion that one lawyer can represent everybody's interests. In many cases, the actual signing of the documents and the closing will take place in the seller's lawyer's office. Ask your lawyer to be present with you on that day and be sure, once again, that you have a clear understanding as to just what his fee will be for the representation. (In many Western states, title and escrow companies do the work of the closing and the buyer and seller split the fee.)

The bank or lender will be represented at the closing and will present the loan charges. There may be an origination fee for the processing of the mortgage application, credit reports, notary service, and preparing papers. These charges may be billed to you as ''miscellaneous fees.'' Whatever these charges are called, be sure you aren't paying for the same services twice under different names. If the lender requires an appraisal of the house and a survey of the property before he grants the loan, you will also be charged for these services. If you have had an appraisal done before you decided to buy the house, check to see if your lender will take a written report from your appraiser. Whatever the circumstances, if you pay for the lender's appraiser to make a report, you should have the benefit of a copy of it in writing. A survey may be avoidable. If the seller has a survey that is less than five years old, and has made no changes to the property, ask the lender to accept it rather than having a new survey made.

Title Examination and Title Insurance

Lenders will frequently ask for a title examination and title insurance. They want to be sure that the seller is free to transfer the property and that there are no hidden claims or liens against it. In some areas of the country, the seller pays for the title examination and search. In most instances, title companies will perform the search and issue the title insurance, a one-time premium. Most often, the cost of the search and of the insurance are paid by the buyer, even though they are essentially a protection for the lender. If the lender designates the use of a particular title company and you're paying the bill, check with other firms to be sure the fees quoted by the lender or his recommended company are competitive.

You should also ask the seller if the house you are about to buy has been insured by a title company in the last two to ten years. If it has, you may be eligible for a reduced rate (reissue rate) that could save you a good deal of money on the premium. Remember, you are buying the title insurance policy for the lender. If you want an owner's policy to protect yourself, ask for a simultaneous policy. The rate for the two policies purchased together will be less than if you purchased them separately.

When you get the Title Examination Report, ask your lawyer to go over it carefully, especially the Schedule B section of the report. It lists the exceptions that the title insurance will not cover. Standard exceptions are listed and there is space to type in exceptions that pertain to the piece of property you plan to buy. There may be restrictive covenants that are ancient, like not being able to raise farm animals on the land—which you probably had no intention of doing. But if those covenants restrict the type of architecture permitted or otherwise limit your use of the property, you should know about them now.

If the exceptions include *easements* that allow utility companies to come onto your land to maintain drainage ditches or telephone wires, or if anyone has a *right-of-way* through your property, you should know about these now also. One standard exception that might be troublesome is called *mechanic's liens*. This means claims that may be filed by persons who did work on a house but weren't paid for it. If you have any reason to suspect that a builder may not have paid his subcontractors, or see that substantial refurbishing has been done to an old house to ready it for sale, try to get that exception removed.

Your lawyer should be your best guide to be sure the title search and insurance you've paid for are clear, and that the title is clear. That's exactly why you bought them.

THE WALK-THROUGH BEFORE CLOSING

Before you get to Closing Day, you will want to do a final walk-through to be sure that all of the problems you've discussed with the seller have been corrected. In a new house, builders usually conduct a walk-through with the buyer to take note of any minor defects and any items to be completed or repaired. For your protection, it would be wise to take a building inspector along on your final walk-through. This may cost around $100, but it can save you many times that if you've registered all complaints with your builder before going to settlement.

If you're buying an old house, you have probably had an appraiser go over it with you. Ask him to go along for your final inspection before the closing. Go over particularly all of the repairs or removal of unwanted objects, or the needed service to appliances, that were detailed in your contract of sale. If you find anything drastically wrong this time around, it's not too late to try to negotiate its correction—but be sure it involves enough money to haggle over at the last minute. Also, you might find that one person's trash is another's treasure. One couple we heard about were so happy with the meticulously kept home they were moving into that they'd never noticed, until the final day, a heap of rotting garbage beside the backyard barbecue. When the former owners were called to task about it, their feelings were deeply hurt. They couldn't understand anyone not wanting their precious compost heap.

THE BUYER'S RESPONSIBILITIES

As the buyer, you may sense by now that your greatest responsibility at the closing will be to take along your checkbook. Specifically, your responsibilities will be very close to the list that follows:

• You'll be expected to pay for the *survey,* if one was needed.

• You'll be expected to pay for the *title search* and *title insurance* if that is the practice in your area. Be sure you have a policy for yourself as well as for the lender. Have the results of the title search with you.

• You'll be expected to pay your portion for any *goods and services* that have been purchased in advance. These might include heating fuel, water, sewage rental, or garbage collection, for example.

• You should have a copy of the *contract of sale* with you to be sure all the previous agreements are clear.

• Take along any notes you made previously on your *final walk-through,* to be sure they have been or will be corrected by the owner. In buying a new house, it would be wise to have these notes in writing, with a copy for the builder and for your records.

• You will be expected to pay your portion of *real estate taxes.* If they have been paid in advance for a year, your portion would be calculated for the part of the year you will occupy the house.

• It will be your lawyer's responsibility to see that the *deed* (the legal document that says you own the house) conforms to the contract of sale.

• It will also be his responsibility to see that the *mortgage terms* are stated as agreed, including any reference to prepayment privileges and penalties for missed payments. These should be clearly spelled out.

• You will be required to have a *hazard insurance policy* at the time of the closing, either as a transfer from the present owner, an independent policy, or a policy through the lender. You'll have to pay that premium in advance.

THE SELLER'S RESPONSIBILITIES

The seller, expecting to get reimbursed for monies he has spent for goods and services, should come prepared with documentation of those expenses:

• He should have a verified reading of the *heating fuel* on hand and a receipted bill showing how much he paid in unit cost for the fuel.

• He should have a receipted bill for *taxes paid* that clearly states the time covered by the payment.

• He should have receipted *water and/or sewage* bills and a statement of the payment date and time covered for the service.

• He should have a receipted bill for *garbage collection* if it is paid in advance.

• If the title search shows any *liens or judgments* outstanding, the seller should be prepared to settle those before any closing papers are signed.

• He should have with him his copy of the *contract of sale*, which should be gone over item by item.

• He should (if a builder) have all *warranties* at the closing to deliver to the purchaser.

• If the buyer is purchasing the house subject to an existing mortgage, there should be proof from the seller showing just how much the *mortgage* has been reduced, the date to which the interest has been paid, and the date on which the mortgage must be paid up.

• He should have the *deed* which conforms to the contract of sale agreement that has been recorded, or will be, at the county courthouse.

• He should provide receipts for all *extras* the buyer agreed to purchase, whether it's fireplace accessories or kitchen appliances.

THE LENDER'S RESPONSIBILITIES

The lender has been handling the processing of the financing of your mortgage and, in some instances, has incurred several of the closing costs in the process. He should have ready any and all documents pertaining to that transaction.

• He should have ready the *mortgage agreement* that clearly states the down payment, the interest rate, points charged, if any, the term of the mortgage in years, and the size of the mortgage. This document should spell out due dates for payments and should clearly state what is included in the monthly payment, such as property taxes, or home insurance if you've taken it through the lender.

• Be sure the mortgage agreement you receive details any arrangements you've made concerning *prepayments,* and the grace period and penalties for *late payments.*

• The lender should supply you with a detailed list of *closing costs* he has incurred in the preparation of the mortgage —if he didn't supply them at your request one full business day before the closing.

• If there are any *deposits required* or an *escrow account* set up for any taxes or other assessments, he should give you a firm understanding of what the account will be used for, and whether the deposit will draw interest, an arrangement some states require. If it won't, see if it's possible for you to put your deposit in a savings account which the bank has privilege to draw upon when payments are due.

NEGOTIABLE RESPONSIBILITIES

There is not likely to be much room for negotiation on several closing items. Property taxes are fixed; the appraisal fee won't be likely to vary greatly from one appraiser to another; the bank's credit report fee and the survey fee are fairly well established in any given area.

These are some of the fees you might try to cut or share:

• You can shop for the best insurance policies if the lender doesn't insist you take them through his institution. If he does, consider that a minus when you judge his services.

• If you're dealing with a commercial bank or a savings bank where you keep your account, it's possible the bank's charge for processing your mortgage application can be held to their minimum for good customers.

• Check with your lawyer to see if you might be able to share such costs as a survey, the title search, a termite inspection, or local recording fees and transfer taxes. The HUD booklet *Settlement Costs* advises, "Such negotiations depend upon such factors as how eager the seller is to sell and you are to buy, the quality of the house . . . how long [it] has been on the market, whether other potential buyers are interested."

• Check with care when a lender recommends a particular title insurance company, an appraiser, or a surveyor. Be sure their prices are competitive with others who are equally qualified to do the job.

• It's a lot of money you're spending. Being careful, checking out all costs, asking if this cost is necessary, are all part of shopping and negotiating wisely. Don't think anyone will judge you as trying to do them in if you ask above-board questions, and proceed with the thought of not leaving any means to saving unexplored.

LEGALITIES FOR SINGLES, COUPLES

While most lending institutions think of single persons or families as home purchasers, there are a growing number of unmarried persons living together who are choosing to invest their pooled funds in a home purchase. All the laws and customs that govern property rights through marriage are not yet sufficiently applicable to protect unmarried partners. Some of the people we talked to had just gone along on faith that they would stay together, and some of them eventually married after they'd bought their homes.

Faith is beautiful, but it really isn't adequate protection for the investment in a home. It may seem hazardous to a relationship to sit in a lawyer's office and discuss a contract that spells out rights, privileges, and responsibilities of joint ownership in case of a breakup or the death of one of the partners, but it is necessary. As one interviewee told us, "Talking it all over with a lawyer didn't horrify me half so much as the thought of Len's mother being able to claim his half of the house should he die."

Your contract should spell out financial responsibilities and, if the deed is in both your names, the laws governing joint property should be explored. They vary widely from state to state. The most equitable joint ownership should provide for the right of survival. That is, whoever survives get the home. The contract should also cover the possibility that the relationship might be broken, and provision should be made for who buys whose half of the house.

Finding understanding lawyers and lenders should not be difficult. The same objective consideration that is given to married couples where husband and wife both work will be given to any two people who are wage earners.

Just as you scout around for the right house in the right neighborhood, you may have to find the best lawyer to work with you, preferably one who's worked on some marriage contracts. The important thing is to work out an equitable, protective arrangement for and with each other.

INSURANCE: HOW MUCH AND WHAT KIND?

In addition to the hazard insurance you are required to have at the time of the closing—which is in effect to protect the lender —you, who have been through a long search for your home, will want to protect your own investment. Immediately.

The most common provision for a wide variety of protection is through a homeowner's policy. Shop for one carefully. Some package policies may include more protection than you need.

If you're moving into a new community, ask friends and neighbors for the name of an insurance agent they know and respect. You can also check your bank or the lawyer you used. Try to deal with someone who is experienced and knows the area well. A reputable agent will be glad to sit down with you and discuss your needs in relationship to your house and the area.

Try to get a fair idea of what it would cost to replace your home should it be destroyed. If you've used an appraiser in judging your house, he should be able to give you a fairly accurate evaluation. Ask your builder what it would cost to build the house you bought *today*. Your insurance agent will also be familiar with costs of house repairs and building trends in the area. Check with him about what it would cost to repair or rebuild a house similar to yours.

The reason it's important to know the value of your house (not including the land it's on) is that you must have it insured for 80 percent of its value at the time of a loss in order to be compensated in full. Otherwise, your insurance would pay only for the depreciated value of your house, not for the actual replacement cost. And it would certainly cost more to build your house today than it would have cost ten years ago.

There are three types of homeowners' policies and they differ primarily in the kinds of perils (that's insurance-ese for dangers) they protect you against. The appeal of the homeowners' policies is that you have only one policy and one premium to pay, and this wide variety of protection costs you less than it would if the same coverages were bought in separate policies.

The three basic policies and what they cover—and don't cover—are outlined briefly below to provide a basic understanding between you and your insurance agent:

The Basic Form (HO-1) is the least expensive one. It covers, as it says, the eleven most likely perils:

1. Fire and lightning.
2. Wind and hail.
3. Explosion.
4. Riot.
5. Aircraft.
6. Vehicles.
7. Smoke.
8. Vandalism.
9. Theft (with the exception of credit cards, checks, pets, boats, and trailers when they're away from the insured premises).
10. Breakage of glass.
11. Loss of property removed from the premises, endangered by fire or other perils.

Also included are:

- Additional living expenses if the house is so severely damaged that it cannot be occupied. (This would cover the cost of hotels, motels, and restaurant meals.)
- Personal liability, which covers a claim against you for damages from someone injured by you in an accident off your property.
- Personal medical payments for others who might injure themselves on your property.
- Damage to property of others. If your budding Little Leaguer hits a neighbor's window, you're covered.

The Broad Form (HO-2) covers *everything* listed above, plus five additional perils:

1. Falling objects.
2. Weight of ice, snow, and sleet.
3. Collapse of building.
4. Accidental damage to steam or hot-water heating systems; accidental leakage within a plumbing, heating, or air-conditioning system, including freezing of these systems.
5. Certain accidents caused by or involving electrical appliances.

Comprehensive Form (HO-5) is the expensive one, often called the "all risk" policy. It covers all perils except earthquake, landslide, floods of various kinds, backing up of sewers, seepage, war, and nuclear radiation.

In buying a homeowner's policy, the homeowner decides the amount of coverage he wants on his home. On this basis, the amount on appurtenant structures (detached garage, tool shed), personal property and additional living expenses are determined at 10 percent, 50 percent, and 20 percent, respectively. If you have a homeowner's policy on a $60,000 house, the home would be insured for $48,000 (80 percent). The appurtenant structures would be insured for $4,800, your personal property for $24,000, and your additional living expenses for $9,600.

Personal property losses must be verified and their value assessed. Now that you're getting ready to move, it's as good a time as any to make a list of the appearance, condition, and value of your possessions. Keep a copy of your inventory in a safe, fireproof place. As you saw above, your personal possessions, under a homeowner's policy, are automatically insured for 50 percent of the amount of insurance on your home. If you possess some items or collections of great value, ask your insurance agent about additional coverage.

You'll want to get insurance immediately, before you move into the home, if possible. When you get your policy and tuck it away as everyone does, put a reminder somewhere, where you're sure to find it, that says, "Review and update home insurance policy every two years."

6

Making the Move

You've passed the closing day on your new home. Your next move is *the move*. It is, without argument, a big job, but one you might dread less if you take the attitude of one of our young wives who declared, "I just love to move. It's the best excuse for getting rid of all that junk we've accumulated." If you think of moving not so much as a chore but as a whole new beginning, it can get you through the seemingly endless job of sorting and packing.

PLANNING THE MOVE

Statistics say that if you have a choice in the timing of your move, you should avoid the summer months, mid-June to the first of September. About 60 percent of moves are made at that time of year, moving accommodations are harder to get, and you will probably face higher rates. Also avoid the first and last days of any month. That's when most leases run out and there's a rush on those days for moving vehicles.

The Tony Skorupskis, who moved from the East Coast to the

West Coast at the time the January 1978 snowstorm paralyzed much of the Midwest, would disagree with those statistics and add that you should try to avoid extreme weather conditions. They spent a night with thousands of other stranded passengers in Chicago's O'Hare Airport and several more hours in Denver, before they arrived with their sleeping bags and most-needed luggage in San Francisco. To add insult to injury, they found out two weeks later that the motor on the moving van carrying their household goods had blown out somewhere in Arkansas.

If your move is to be one of great distance, try to set a date (or dates) as soon as possible so you can shop for a moving company and make a firm arrangement with the one you choose. Four to six weeks' advance notice is what the large, interstate (from one state to another) companies prefer.

Advance planning will give you an opportunity to have one or more moving firms come in, look over your possessions to be moved, and give you an estimated cost of services. Choose a firm that has a solid reputation, especially if yours is an interstate move. The Interstate Commerce Commission (ICC) regulates all interstate moving firms and sets the rates, determined by the weight of the goods and the distance moved plus any special services such as packing, unpacking, or storage. *Intrastate* movers move only within the borders of one state, and are usually controlled by a state agency. Local movers, however, operate without any government regulations, and they will either charge a flat rate or an hourly fee. Even if your move is across town, the more notice you can give a mover, the more likely you are to get service when it suits you best.

Having a target date well in advance of moving day can also help you. If you're someone who's looking forward to "getting rid of all that junk," remember that some of it may represent nostalgia and it may take you longer to part with it than you thought. Regardless of the distance of your move, begin an inventory of your possessions. By numbering your boxes and furniture to match the inventory, you can simplify checking against losses or missing pieces when you arrive at your destination. Also, remember that this inventory will serve as a record of your possessions that you will want to have filed with your home-owner's insurance policy.

Make the decision now, whether you are going to have the moving company do all the packing and unpacking, and unhooking and hooking up your appliances. This is by far the easiest way to move. It's also the most expensive. If this is your decision, you can eliminate those items numbered (1) on checklists 6a, 6b, and 6c, which will help you prepare for the move. The chores have been divided into those to be done well in advance, the week before, and the day before moving.

PETS, PLANTS, AND OTHER HARD-TO-MOVE POSSESSIONS

Pets, if they can't be taken with you by car or by air, will need to have special shipping arrangements made for them. Most important, if you are moving to another state or even to another community, check any state or local regulations relating to pet ownership or pet entry. Check these well in advance of your move so you can obtain from your veterinarian any health certificates necessary and apply for entry permits if they are needed. The moving company you use may be able to supply you with information on regulations. Especially if the pet belongs to children, it is important that you be sure their pet can be with them in a strange, new place.

Plants, unless they are relatively small and traveling a short distance, are not good movers. The movers will take them in their vans but will warn you that they may not thrive without water and sunlight if it's a long trip. You may be able to pack a box of African violets and take them with you by car or plane, but if you have a towering *dieffenbachia,* try to think of someone who will love it as you did and make them a present of it.

Large mirrors, glass tabletops, and fragile screens really need special packaging. Ask your movers to bring the proper materials along for packing such breakables.

THE COSTS OF MOVING

The Bill of Lading will have on it any charges that you have agreed to for packing, unpacking, special pickups such as piano moving, and the weight of the truck prior to the loading of your goods. The Bill of Lading will also have a space on it where you must select the valuation you wish for your goods. If the space provided is not written in, your goods will be moved at a declared value equal to the weight of the shipment in pounds multiplied by $1.25. If you write in the lump-sum value you choose, it must be equal to or more than the pound weight of your shipment times $1.25. In both instances, you will be charged 50¢ per $100 of the total value. The extent of the protection you get free is 60¢ per pound. That means that if a lamp base weighing four pounds gets broken, the reimbursement to you would be only $2.40. However, if you'd insured it at $1.25 per pound, you would get $5.00. Obviously you should not pack money, jewelry, important papers, valuable personal items—or really expensive lamps or breakables.

Prior to moving day you will have had an "Estimated Cost of Services," based on the moving company's visual knowledge of what you plan to move and the distance involved. You really won't know the actual cost until your goods have been placed on the van and weighed. (The movers will weigh the van before they load your goods on it and then again afterward. The difference is the weight of your shipment.) You are required by law to pay the moving fee by cash, certified check, traveler's check, or money order before the van man can unload your goods. If the total charge exceeds the estimate by more than 10 percent, the mover is required by the Interstate Commerce Commission to deliver your goods upon payment of the estimated charges (which you should have in a safe check form) plus 10 percent, which you can safely have in cash. You will then have fifteen working days to pay the balance on the shipment, but packing and insurance charges should be added to the original payment.

You may ask to make other arrangements for payment, such as the use of a credit card, which has the advantage of giving you an opportunity to check over the condition of your goods carefully before you hand out cash.

You will protect yourself against further costs by planning to be on hand to receive the shipment. The mover is required to wait only three hours for you to accept your goods, and less time if your move is under 200 miles. If the mover is unable to deliver within the free waiting time, he may place your goods in storage and you will be charged for the storage and redelivery.

Your presence and careful checking as the goods are unloaded will also protect you from losses, or damaged goods. The driver or some representative of the moving company will have made an inventory of your goods and noted any unusual conditions. As your things are unpacked, you should be checking the inventory item by item and noting any damages or missing items. Make notations of losses or damages on both your and the driver's copy of the inventory. If you enter a claim, the ICC requires the mover to answer that claim in thirty days.

As you're checking the inventory, keep an eye on where furniture and boxes are being placed. You don't want to end up with kitchen dishes in a bedroom. There'll be plenty to do without moving boxes a second time. Best to make up some beds, have a light supper, and get a good night's sleep.

DO-IT-YOURSELF MOVING

If your move is a relatively short one, you may be able to accomplish it with a rented haul-it-yourself truck or trailer. Before you tackle a move yourself, be sure you have ample time at both ends of the haul so you won't have to do an excessive amount of heavy lifting for, say, twelve or fourteen hours in any one day. If you have a week to get out of your present living quarters and have possession of your new home, you can move small things, a few at a time, by car and enlist some help, paid or volunteer, for the moving of the big pieces.

When you move piecemeal, be certain that your home is secure and fitted with good, new window and door locks. Even petty thieves or just curious mischief-makers have a way of knowing when a house is unlived in.

If you plan a do-it-yourself move, be sure it will save you money. It's possible that a one-man, large-truck local mover would be just as cheap as a haul-it-yourself rental for the length of time you may need it. Also, you may have to rent some padding and buy some special cartons for packing pictures, mirrors, and the like. Do you have insurance that would cover any damage to goods during the move? The local mover probably does carry such a policy. Shop, compare, ask others who have done a move themselves, and be sure, above all, that you're really saving money.

KEEP A RECORD OF MOVING EXPENSES

Frequently, companies that have asked an employee to come and work for them in a location that necessitates a move for the employee, will reimburse moving expenses. Before you lose track of airline tickets, automobile expenses, hotels and meals, and the eventual expenses of moving your goods, get them all in one keepable folder. If your company reimburses you in part or in full for moving expenses, you must include that reimbursement, for tax purposes, in your gross income in the year in which it was paid to you.

You can qualify for tax deductions of moving expenses if your move was caused by a change in the location of your employment—either as a result of a transfer by your present employer or by your acceptance of a new job. To deduct reasonable moving expenses, these conditions must be met:

1. The change in job location requires you to commute at least thirty-five miles *farther* to work than if you had not moved.
2. The move occurs within one year of the date you begin work at the new location.

3. You work full-time (for any employer) in the general vicinity of the new location for at least thirty-nine weeks during the twelve-month period following the move.

If you are self-employed, these rules also apply, except that you are required to work at the new location for seventy-eight weeks, of which thirty-nine must be during the first twelve-month period following the move.

Though not all of the information on Checklist 6d may be used in making out your tax return, it will be a safeguard for you or your accountant to have in one place the receipts or records of these expenses that pertain to your move.

If you have done your own moving but feel you may qualify for a tax deduction, keep a record of all rentals and other expenses necessary to the move. Between now and tax-reporting time, it might be helpful to you to pick up a copy of the booklet entitled, *Tax Information on Moving Expenses*, Internal Revenue Service Publication 521 (10-72). A copy may be obtained from the nearest office of the Internal Revenue Service.

Checklist 6a. A PLAN FOR MOVING

(1) = you can ignore these jobs if you're hiring your packing done
(D) = these are important if you're moving to a new town or city
(M) = these must be done for any move

Set aside a table that will serve now as a place to stack discards until you can either throw them away or give them away, such as books to a secondhand store, old clothing and bric-a-brac to a thrift shop or a church rummage sale. Most charities will pick up donations. Later this can become your packing center.

Check each item off as it gets done

_____

(D) Start your possessions inventory.   _____
(D) Begin now to deplete your supply of canned and frozen foods. Canned goods are heavy and frozen foods will survive no more than a short move.   _____
(M) Get a supply of change of address cards from your post office.   _____
(M) Notify services of your moving date:

Telephone	_____
Post Office	_____
Electric and/or gas	_____
Water	_____
Fuel	_____

(M) Send change-of-address notices to all publications as soon as possible. They need at least four weeks' notice.   _____
(1) Start to gather sturdy cartons, such as liquor boxes. Get some tissue paper, unprinted newsprint (if available), sturdy tape and felt marking pencils. Never use printed newspaper except as outside packing or wrapping. The ink will stain dishes.   _____
(D) Get medical records together and ask your present doctors to refer you to a counterpart in your new place of residence.

Doctors	_____
Dentist	_____
Ophthalmologist	_____
Other	_____

(D) Check with your bank to arrange transfer of funds and establishment of credit in your new place of residence.   _____
(D) If children are involved, arrange to have their school records available for transfer to new schools.   _____
(D) Arrange a last-week going-over for the car or, if not driving, make travel reservations.   _____
(M) Arrange to have any furnishings such as drapes and rugs

cleaned. If your move is local, they can be delivered to your new address; if it's distant, they should be wrapped for packing.   _____

(1) Start packing such things as out-of-season clothes, good silver, china. Label boxes with contents and where they should be placed in the new home (kitchen, bedroom, etc.)   _____

(1) Keep packing.
Keep adding to your possessions inventory.   _____

Check list 6b. LAST-WEEK PLANNING

(M) Have all appliances disconnected so they can be emptied and/or wiped clean and dry.   _____

(M) Launder all soiled clothing before the washing machine is disconnected.   _____

(D) Pack an "It'll be nice when we get there" box to go with you, with:

Some paper or plastic eating utensils   _____
A saucepan   _____
Instant coffee or tea   _____
A flashlight   _____
Soap, washcloths, and towels   _____
Night clothes   _____
Cosmetics   _____
Razor   _____
One change of clothing   _____
Children's favorite toys   _____

(Think of this box, or bag, as an emergency kit you could live out of in case an ice storm prevents the movers from moving on the planned day.)

(M) Check contents of drawers. (If you plan to leave light clothing in drawers, that's fine. Remove anything spill-able.)   _____

(M) If you must carry medicines or other liquid, tape the cap securely and overwrap with a plastic bag securely fas-tened.   _____

(M) Throw away any flammable items such as cleaning fluids. (They're not worth the chance of moving.)   _____

Checklist 6c. THE DAY BEFORE THE MOVE

(1)   Have everything packed except such items as large mirrors and glass tabletops. (leave these to the movers).   _____

(M)   Strip beds.   _____

(M)   Double-check that all fragile items are clearly marked.   _____

(M)   Double-check every cabinet, closet, nook, and cranny to be sure nothing's left behind.   _____

(D)   Try not to use radios or television sets for several hours before the movers are due. They should not be warm for moving.   _____

(M)   Go out for dinner, even if it's just for a hamburger, and try to spend the night with friends.   _____

(B)   The day of the move, be on hand to greet the movers, sign an inventory if it's an interstate move, and approve and sign the Bill of Lading. (Don't leave the premises until all your possessions are loaded and ready to go.)   _____

Checklist 6d. MOVING EXPENSES

Check to be sure
these are on hand

House-hunting expenses prior to the move

Transportation costs (one trip for you and your family)

    Air, bus, or train fare (keep ticket receipts)   _____

    Transportation to and from airports or stations   _____

    Automobile (actual out-of-pocket expenses for gas, oil, tolls, and repairs)—check current mileage allowance with IRS (keep receipts)   _____

Meals while on the trip (keep receipts)   _____

Lodging while on the trip (keep receipts)   _____

Home-purchasing expenses

    Attorney's fees   _____

    Title search fee   _____

    Survey fee   _____

    Points paid   _____

    Escrow fees   _____

    Transfer taxes   _____

    Property taxes assumed in the year of the move   _____

    Appraiser fee   _____

    Breakdown of any other closing costs

_____   _____

_____   _____

_____   _____

Moving expenses
Bill of lading which will show all moving charges made to you   _____
Inventory which will be a record of damages or losses   _____
Record of moving company's payment for damages or losses,
  if any   _____
Weight certificate   _____
Packing and unpacking certificate, if that service was provided
  by the moving company   _____
Any additional expenses connected with the move

_____   _____
_____   _____
_____   _____

Transportation
  Air, bus, or train fare   _____
  Transportation to airports or stations   _____
  Meals enroute   _____
  Lodging enroute   _____

Temporary living expenses (while looking for home)
  Meals   _____
  Lodging   _____

NOTES

_____

_____

_____

_____

_____

_____

_____

7

Settling In

RELAX AND ENJOY IT, IF ONLY TEMPORARILY

One new-home buyer had this piece of advice: "For the first week you're in your new home, try to forget the curtains you have to make, the painting that has to be done, that window that has to be unstuck, and all the rest of the long list of things you dream of doing." Even if relaxing and enjoying the end of a long search means relaxing in the only room that's liveable, do it. There are plenty of tomorrows to plan the decor and there will be some basic needs you will probably have to take care of for pure business reasons. Live with some unpacked boxes and some misplaced furniture for a while, especially if you want to have some floors sanded and finished before you put down rugs or move big furniture pieces into place. Skip hanging the clean drapes until you've painted the room, if that's part of your master plan. If you've moved into an old house or are undertaking a renovation project, you'll probably be doing a lot of chipping and stripping before you're ready for finishing touches. Your books, dishes, silver, and extra linens will all be better protected from the dust and dirt if they stay securely packed as moved.

However, there are some basic things to be done right away. The following list is a reminder of these necessities:

- Put all your documents and receipts pertaining to the purchase of your home and your moving expenses in one safe place, preferably a safe-deposit box. Pay particular attention to this if your move has been made at the end of the year. Your January estimated taxes or even the Internal Revenue Service's annual demand on April 15 will seem to come very soon on the heels of all the disruption you've been through. If you've moved into a new home, put your new-home warranty with your valuable papers.

- Check with the post office to see if any mail has accumulated for you, and let them know you're now in residence and ready for regular deliveries.

- Check requirements for automobile registration and operator's licenses. There may be a time limit on making those transferable. While you're about it, check to see if you need to make any changes in your automobile insurance.

- Check in at the bank you plan to use. Have all of your funds been transferred? Do you need to order new checks? Is your name correctly spelled on their records? Is your address correct? Has your credit rating been established?

- Check in with any doctors or dentists who have been recommended to you. It's hardly necessary to go see them right away if all is well, but it will be comforting to know they are there and practicing, in case of emergency.

- If there's an election coming up soon, register so you will be eligible to vote.

- Get the phone number of the local fire department and police and put them in an easily accessible place in your phone book.

- Are the utilities and phones already connected?

- Are all of your major appliances hooked up and in good working order?

- If you've moved into a newly built house and begin to notice some unfinished work or some nonworking doors, windows, or appliances, start a list. You will have to put these *in writing* to your builder to get him to make good on them.

- Locate the nearest supermarket and the nearest small grocery store. As you get acquainted, these may not be your selected shopping places, but it's good to know where to go for such staples as bread and milk.

- If your move has been made during a school year, check in with the school to see that your children are properly registered and ready to begin classes as soon as possible. If you have preschool children, check nursery classes and/or line up some recommended baby-sitters. Days off and nights out may be high on your priority list now.

MAKING FRIENDS IN THE COMMUNITY

You may feel you have so much to do to complete the move that you don't have time for socializing. And maybe you don't think of yourself as a great socializer. Sooner or later, however, it's going to be necessary for you to have some stalwart friends among the tradespeople in your town. The best people to direct you to the well-equipped hardware store, the most competent plumber, the most capable electrician, and the most reliable garage mechanic are the people who have lived in the town. Getting to know your close neighbors and making acquaintance with people you meet through a church or synagogue will help in your detective work of finding the people who will be most help to you in the next weeks and months. No one expects you to be entertaining formally right off, but you won't get much help from anyone if you give the impression of being a recluse.

Check out the social or community organizations that serve interests similar to your own. Find out about the recreational facilities and any specialized clubs you might like to join. If you're a tennis buff, for instance, and pretty good at it, you'll want to find someone who's in your competitive class.

If you have children, remember that they too have social needs that may be even stronger than yours. Children can feel insecure in new surroundings and need some continuity of the interests they had "back home." Swimmers might find it at the local "Y." A child who loves to play an instrument might find it in a school orchestra. A singer might get great pleasure out of being in the church choir.

If you're moving from a city to a small or suburban community, there may be several attractions through the local historical society, tours through the garden clubs, or unusual hobby groups. Getting acquainted in a smaller community can be a little like being a tourist on vacation. If you're a reader, you'll want to check out the local library and apply for lending cards for each member of the family. Children can be guided to their athletic interests. If you've a budding Johnny Bench, he might not make the starting lineup the first year out in the Little League, but he'll be making friends with people who share his interests.

There are "welcome wagons" operating in almost every community in the country. They'll be listed in the advertising pages of your phone book under Welcoming Services. If you think that isn't your cup of tea, don't turn it down until you've seen what they have to offer. Or ask some new neighbors how they felt about the service offered in that community. You've nothing to lose and it might be a new experience. If they did nothing else but introduce you to some good, inexpensive restaurants, that would be a plus. There will be those times in the weeks ahead when the paint odor is too strong for you to stay in the house or you simply haven't the energy left to boil an egg.

DO-IT-YOURSELF BUT DON'T INUNDATE YOURSELF

Doing-it-yourself has become a way of life for many young men and women for the very basic reason that it can save money. And a lot of people really enjoy the accomplishment of getting a perfect match on the wallpaper or removing enough coats of paint to get down to the beautiful old oak door. There's enormous satisfaction in standing back and admiring the perfect job you did of laying tiles on your kitchen floor. Even if it isn't exactly perfect, there is still satisfaction in the "I did it myself" feeling.

There is also the fact that skilled workpeople are hard to get. Often the plumber will keep you on an indefinite waiting list for weeks, and paperhanger-painters are frequently more concerned with getting the job done in a hurry rather than doing it well.

If you are planning a lot of do-it-yourself work, give yourself a reasonable timetable. That's what's really at the base of the warning, "Don't inundate yourself." If you have several jobs ahead, start a priority list. Amy and Lew Scotton said, "Wherever we move, we always get floors in good condition first." Nancy and Bill Doris say they always get the walls painted or papered first. It really doesn't matter—there will be people who believe they can live with any inconvenience just so the kitchen is in good working order. Your priorities are yours alone. Make them to suit you and the jobs that your home needs.

There are some general rules that experienced do-it-yourselfers recommend. Give them fair consideration; they all evolved out of good and bad experiences:

1. Do only those jobs that you feel qualified to do. If there are jobs you want to tackle without adequate know-how, you have two avenues to follow. Get someone who is qualified to help you and show you how, or go to school and learn how. Many high schools and community colleges offer courses on home repairs. Learning the right way to wire a lamp or repair house siding or make some simple plumbing changes is like taking insurance that the job will come out right.

2. Don't try to save money on materials. A low grade of paint or a warped piece of wood is no bargain, and can reduce any feeling of accomplishment to bitter disappointment.

3. Overestimate the time it will take you to do any given job. Give yourself time to ask questions, locate the right materials, and proceed methodically with the job so you can enjoy it.

4. Don't proceed with any job like wiring or plumbing or putting an addition on your house until you check the local zoning laws and the local building codes. Any installation you make that is in violation of local rules and regulations can jeopardize the effectiveness of your home insurance.

5. If the job you're about to do is largely decorative, have a plan, a decorating plan. You may paint a bedroom wall a given shade of blue because you like the color and spend the next year trying to find a fabric for curtains that won't fight with that lovely blue.

6. Don't buy highly specialized tools; try to rent them instead. But do have a list of basic tools you need and will use over and over again. Let parents and friends and any doting relatives know that you'd rather have a multipurpose wrench than a ginger-jar lamp for a housewarming present.

7. Take a day off to find out about the newest do-it-yourself materials available for the job you plan. Improvements are constantly being made in the materials and the methods for doing all sorts of jobs around the house. Think what an innovation prepasted wallpaper was. Take a day off from doing home improvements and shop a large home-supplies store. You might find there's an easier way to do most any job you have in mind.

8. Tackle early in the game those jobs that have to do with the maintenance of your house or the saving of energy. A leaky roof to repair, weather stripping to apply, puttying loose windowpanes, or adding insulation to the attic isn't half so glamorous as unearthing a beautiful old walnut balustrade. But the balustrade will cost you nothing if it sits there overlaid with irreverent paint. A leaky roof or ill-fitting windows will cost you money in precious fuel.

9. Do try to avoid potentially dangerous jobs. If the fuel lines need repair or electric circuits are in need of complete overhaul, get an expert on the job. If you're using power tools or a flame torch to burn off old paint, be particularly careful of potential hazards.

10. Be an instruction or label reader. If you're using a new product, trust that the manufacturer wants you to know how to use it successfully and properly.

And don't forget to keep reviewing that list of priorities. You may discover another "first" as you go along.

GETTING TO KNOW YOUR NEW HOUSE

Houses, like children, tend to need more care and attention than you might have imagined. A gutter or a leader might have meant nothing to you six months ago, but now you'll have to be aware that they, like every part of your house, demand constant checking. One person we talked with said, "I go to my doctor for an annual checkup but I have to give my house a checkup at least once a month to know what condition it's in. And sometimes a monthly check doesn't do it." The most often repeated advice from home owners was, "Don't let the little things go. A drip in the attic might not bother you, but if it isn't taken care of when it's a drip it'll become a flood."

If you buy a new home, one of the booklets you'll be given by your builder will be devoted to telling you how to maintain your home. Study it just as carefully as you studied the fine print in your mortgage. Builders say that owners, especially first-home owners, run into troubles they think of as defects in the house when they're really responsible because they haven't cared for their home properly. Most first-home owners have come from apartment or house-rental situations and were used to having someone else worry about the drips and the cracks and the misperformance of the hot-water system.

If you've chosen cooperative or condominium ownership for the very reason that someone else will take care of the building's problems, you're partially hiding your head in the sand. Physically, someone else will take care of plumbing repairs and the like. But as co-owner of a cooperative building, don't forget that the care and maintenance of the building has an important bearing on your investment. You should be interested and constantly insistent that the management of the building keep an eye on the maintenance, if not the upgrading, of all the basic systems and the condition of the building.

As an old-home owner you can expect to uncover some eccentricities. You can learn to love a creaking floor in a hallway or it can be a constant irritation. If it's the former, you'd better see if it's something that will lead to future trouble. If the latter, fix it immediately.

One real estate agent told us that the relationship between a house and the owner's ego is a highly emotional affair. To some people, a home might be a refuge; to others, a necessary burden; to some, isolation; to others, a security blanket. Whatever your home means to you, know that you are its master. If you care for it properly, it will serve you well and be all the things *you* want it to be. As one young woman said, "Well, it's sort of a love-hate relationship. You love it really, but you hate it when everything seems to go wrong at once."

You've made a good investment. Guard it with care and it should reward you with handsome and happy returns.

The Home Buyer's Dictionary

When you go house hunting, you'll begin to hear and see words and phrases that may be baffling and may leave you wondering what on earth people are talking about. Other words may sound vaguely familiar, but you may not be exactly sure what they mean. This is a list of commonly used words and phrases that should be helpful as you search for a home. Further details on what they mean can be found in the appropriate chapters of this book.

Because many of these definitions are necessarily interrelated, words IN SMALL CAPITALS are also defined elsewhere, in their alphabetical place.

Because there are many local phrases that creep into use in certain parts of the country, there's space at the end of this section for you to add your own new words. If you hear a word or phrase you don't understand, ask your lawyer or your real estate agent what it means and add it to this general list.

NOTE: In addition to this list you may want to order the booklet *Homeowner's Glossary of Building Terms,* free from U.S. Department of Housing and Urban Development, Washington, DC 20410.

Abstract (of title)—A summary or condensed history of the legal TITLE to a piece of property. It will include previous transfers and any records that may CLOUD the title.

Acceleration clause—A condition in a MORTGAGE that gives the LENDER the right to ask for the balance of the loan to become due immediately. This might be based on missed payments or breach of other conditions of the contract.

Agreement of sale—Also known as purchase agreement, sales agreement, or contract of purchase. It is a written agreement between the BUYER and the SELLER that spells out the terms and conditions under which the buyer agrees to buy and the seller agrees to sell. Usually a small deposit (known as EARNEST MONEY) is put down by the buyer. Both parties sign the agreement.

Amortization—A payment plan, usually in monthly installments, to gradually reduce the principal of the MORTGAGE loan.

Appraisal—An evaluation of a specific property by an expert (APPRAISER) estimated in terms of money. It will reflect the condition of the house and the market value of the property on a given date.

Appraiser—Someone qualified by experience and education to estimate the value of property, based on a thorough examination of that property.

Appreciation—An increase in value; the opposite of DEPRECIATION.

Appurtenance—Something that goes along with the primary building on the property, such as a barn, a tool shed, or an orchard. Homeowners' insurance policies refer to "appurtenant structures."

Assessed value—The money value placed on a property as a basis for taxation.

Assessment—In a CONDOMINIUM, the operating costs charged, usually monthly, to an owner. In a house, a special charge to homeowners made by a local government for a community project, such as a new sewage system, new street improvements, or the like.

Binder—A receipt for a deposit of money paid by the prospective BUYER to the SELLER to secure the right to purchase a property. Related to an AGREEMENT OF SALE.

Broker—A person licensed by the state to assist BUYERS and SELLERS of property.

Building line or setback—Distances from the land's end and/or sides of the lot beyond which you cannot build.

Buyer—The person who plans to purchase or who purchases, in this case, a piece of property.

Caveat—A warning, a notice to beware, and be aware of, a clause in a document.

C C and Rs—The letters stand for covenants, conditions, and restrictions. They define the use you may make of the property and spell out any regulations that may not be violated. Be sure you know if and how these pertain to a piece of property you plan to purchase.

Certificate of title—A document issued by a title company or a lawyer that says the SELLER has the right to the property he is offering for sale.

Closing—The occasion when the BUYER and the SELLER—or their representatives—conclude the transfer of property.

Closing costs—Expenses incurred to complete the transaction of transferring ownership of real estate . For the buyer, these may include the cost of the SURVEY, TITLE SEARCH, TITLE INSURANCE, and other expenses.

Cloud (on title)—An outstanding LIEN or ENCUMBRANCE which means the TITLE to the property is not clear.

Commission—Money paid to a real estate agent or broker by the SELLER for the agent's services in finding a BUYER and completing a sale. Usually the fee is a percentage of the sale price of the property.

Condominium—A form of home ownership in which the owner owns a unit in a multi-unit dwelling and a share of common facilities, such as grounds.

Contingency—A condition spelled out in the AGREEMENT OF SALE that must happen before the agreement is legally binding. The most common contingency allows for the ability of the BUYER to get MORT-GAGE financing.

Contract of Purchase—*See* AGREEMENT OF SALE.

Conventional mortgage—A form of MORTGAGE in which the monthly costs remain the same during the entire repayment period.

Cooperative—A form of home ownership in which the owner occupies a unit in a multi-unit dwelling and owns stock in the corporation owning the dwelling.

Credit report—A report to the LENDER, made at his request, on the credit standing of the borrower/BUYER.

Deed—A legal document used to transfer ownership of property. The deed should include an accurate description of the property being transferred, and it must be registered in the county records office.

Default—Failure to make a MORTGAGE payment or observe other conditions of the mortgage agreement.

Deposit—*See* EARNEST MONEY.

Depreciation—Decline in value of a house or property due to wear, adverse changes in the neighborhood, or any other reason affecting the desirability of the property.

Discount points—*See* POINTS.

Documentary stamps—A state tax, in the form of stamps, required on DEEDS and MORTGAGES when property is transferred from one owner to another.

Down payment—The amount of money that must be paid when, or before, the property is sold.

Earnest money—A deposit of money given to the SELLER by the potential BUYER when the AGREEMENT OF SALE is signed. It says the buyer is serious about buying the property. If the sale goes through, the earnest money is applied to the DOWN PAYMENT. If it doesn't go through, the earnest money may be lost unless the agreement provides specifically the conditions under which it should be returned.

Easement—A right-of-way granted to a person or a company giving access to or over the owner's land. Utility companies often hold easement rights over land.

Encumbrance—A legal right or interest in land that affects a clear TITLE. Encumbrances may include EASEMENT rights, unpaid taxes, LIENS, or restrictive covenants. The BUYER determines whether he wants to purchase with the encumbrances or sees that an encumbrance is removed before he agrees to buy.

Equity—The value of a homeowner's paid-up principal on a MORTGAGE loan minus any debts against the property.

Escrow—The deposit of funds or items of value with a bank or a neutral third party to be used to carry out the real estate transaction or held in custody until all details of the transaction have been fulfilled.

Fee simple—The absolute ownership of property without restriction on transfer of ownership.

FHA (Federal Housing Administration)—Insures MORTGAGE loans made by FHA-approved lenders on homes that meet FHA standards.

Foreclosure—A legal term applied to any of the various methods of enforcing payment of a MORTGAGE debt, frequently a sale by a bank or other LENDER of a property on which payments are in serious DEFAULT.

Graduated-payment mortgage (GPM)—A form of MORTGAGE in which the payments do not become fixed until the sixth year of the repayment period.

Grantee—The BUYER, or the receiver, of a DEED.

Grantor—The SELLER, or the giver, of a DEED.

Interest—A charge made for borrowing money. It is always figured at a percentage rate and is part of the monthly MORTGAGE payment.

Joint tenancy—Joint ownership by two or more persons with RIGHT

OF SURVIVAL. All joint tenants own equal interest and have equal rights in the property.

Lender—A person or institution that grants a loan, in this case a MORTGAGE loan.

Lien—A claim by one person on the property of another as a security for money owed.

Mortgage—A legal claim against real property given by the BUYER (borrower) to the LENDER as security for the money borrowed.

Mortgagee—The LENDER in a MORTGAGE agreement.

Mortgagor—The borrower in a MORTGAGE agreement.

Option—*See* AGREEMENT OF SALE.

Plat—A map or chart of a lot, subdivision, or community drawn up by a SURVEYOR, showing boundary lines, buildings, and EASEMENTS.

Points—Amounts of a *mortgage* loan (one point is 1 percent) charged by a LENDER when other circumstances indicate he needs to raise the yield on his money invested in the loan.

Prepayment—Prepayment of a MORTGAGE loan, or part of it, before the due date. Mortgage agreements often do not permit prepayment, or limit the amount that may be prepaid in any given year.

Principal—The basic amount of the loan, not including interest, any MORTGAGE insurance premiums, or other charges.

Purchase agreement—*See* AGREEMENT OF SALE.

Purchase money mortgage—A MORTGAGE granted directly to the BUYER by the SELLER of the home.

Real estate agent or broker—*See* BROKER.

Realtor—A REAL ESTATE AGENT who is a member of the National Association of Realtors.

Recording fee—A fee charged by the county to record the transfer of TITLE from the SELLER to the BUYER.

Restriction—A limitation upon the use of real property.

Right of survival—The right to acquire the interest of a deceased joint owner. This is the distinguishing feature of a JOINT TENANCY.

Sales agreement—*See* AGREEMENT OF SALE.

Seller—The person who intends to sell or who sells, in this case, a piece of property.

Setback—*See* BUILDING LINE.

Subdivision—Improved or unimproved land divided for the purpose of sale, lease, or financing, now or in the future. Often used to mean a section of land that has been divided into parcels and laid out in lots for construction of homes.

Survey—A map or *plat* made by a licensed SURVEYOR showing exact boundaries and location of a property.

Surveyor—One licensed to draw up a SURVEY of a property.

Tenancy in common—Ownership by two or more persons who hold individual interest in a property. Interests need not be equal, and this ownership is without RIGHT OF SURVIVAL.

Title—A legal document proving the right of ownership to a property.

Title insurance—A one-time-premium insurance that protects LENDERS or BUYERS against loss of their interest in property due to legal defects in the TITLE.

Title search—A check of TITLE records to make sure the BUYER is purchasing property free from LIENS, ENCUMBRANCES, ASSESSMENTS, and other defects in the title.

Zoning—Classification of real property for varying uses.

Zoning ordinances—The acts of an authorized local government establishing building codes and setting forth regulations for property uses.

Other words and phrases important to my house hunting:

Booklets Worth Sending For

Many of the first-home buyers we interviewed said, "Read everything on the subject you can when you're thinking about buying a home." While this book was designed to cover all of the major choices and considerations for first-home buyers, there are several good booklets —some general, some specialized—that we have reviewed and recommend. They are listed below according to the interests they address.

Overall Information

A Home Buyers Guide, 31 pages, 1975.
Especially good information on mortgage planning and closing costs.
50¢ from American Bankers Association, 1120 Connecticut Avenue, NW, Washington, DC 20005.
Home Buyers Guide, 32 pages, 1974.
Excellent guide and information, especially directed to the new-home buyer.
$1.00 from the National Association of Home Builders, 15th and M Streets, NW, Washington, DC 20005.
Wise Home Buying, 28 pages, October 1978, HUD-267-H(8).
Concise, easy-to-read information on making judgments and decisions on old or new homes.

Free from U.S. Department of Housing and Urban Development, 451 7th Street, SW, Room B-258, Washington, DC 20410.

Selecting and Financing a Home, 24 pages, revised September 1977.

Good, simply written information. Easy to understand. Fairly general.

Free from U.S. Department of Agriculture, Room 507A, 14th Street and Independence Avenue, SW, Washington, DC 20250.

Tips on Buying a Home, 13 pages, 1979.

Brief but good reminder of the important steps in home buying.

Free from Council of Better Business Bureaus, 1150 17th Street, NW, Washington, DC 20036. Send stamped, self-addressed #10 envelope.

The Energy-Wise Home Buyer—A Guide to Selecting an Energy Efficient Home, 60 pages, April 1979.

Excellent book for prospective or present home owners. Addresses the problems of selecting an energy-efficient home. Also tells how to make a home more energy-efficient. Could save you $'s on fuel bills.

$2.00 from the Superintendent of Documents, U.S. Government Printing Office, Washington, DC 20402. GPO Stock No. 023-000-00518-2.

Homeowner's Glossary of Building Terms, 14 pages, January 1976, HUD-369-F(3).

If a corbel, a cavity, and a chimney cap are Greek to you, this little booklet will be a handy one to tuck in your pocket when you're talking with a building inspector or an appraiser.

Free from U.S. Department of Housing and Urban Development, 451 7th Street, SW, Room B-258, Washington, DC 20410.

Homebuyer's Information Package, A Guidebook for Buying and Owning a Home, approx. 100 pages, September 1979.

A good, complete workbook, especially its follow-through on responsibility of home ownership.

Price $4.95 from the Superintendent of Documents, U.S. Government Printing Office, Washington, DC 20402. GPO Stock No. 023-000-00508-5.

Especially for Buyers of Mobile Homes

Tips on Buying a Mobile Home, 15 pages, 1978.

Concise, good information on mobile home information.

Free from Council of Better Business Bureaus, 1150 17th Street, NW, Washington, DC 20036. Send stamped, self-addressed #10 envelope.

Quick Facts About the Manufactured Housing Industry.
Just as it says, quick facts about mobile and modular homes.
Free from Manufactured Housing Institute, 1745 Jefferson Davis High-
way, Suite 511, Arlington, VA 22202.

Especially for Buyers of Panelized or Precut Homes

Guide to Manufactured Homes, 100 pages, 1979.
Slick, glossy annual, contains much advertising that serves as a guide
to makers of manufactured homes and house styles.
Good information editorially.
$4.00 from National Association of Home Manufacturers, 6521 Arling-
ton Boulevard, Falls Church, VA 22042

Especially for Condominium Buyers

Condominium Buyers Guide, 31 pages, 1976.
Especially thorough book for condominium buyers, with all possible
pitfalls spelled out.
$1.00 from the National Association of Home Builders, 15th and M
Streets, NW, Washington, DC 20005.
Questions About Condominiums, 48 pages, June 1976, HUD-365-F(3).
Good information, simply presented; includes a vocabulary of condo-
minium-buying terms.
Free from the U.S. Department of Housing and Urban Development,
451 7th Street, SW, Room B-258, Washington, DC 20410.

Especially for Veterans

*To the Home Buying Veteran—A Guide for Veterans Planning to Buy
or Build Homes with a GI Loan.* VA 26-6, 36 pages, revised Febru-
ary 1979.
Guaranteed and Direct Loans for Veterans—Questions and Answers.
VA 26-4, 29 pages, revised December 1978.
Includes list of VA Regional Offices.
Questions and Answers on Specially Adapted Housing for Veterans.
VA 26-69-1, revised February 1979.
Free from regional Veterans Administration offices. Look under U.S.
Government listings in the telephone book or ask at any community
agency office for VA regional office address.

Money Matters

The House-Hunter's Guide, 22 pages, 1977.

A good overall guide to house hunting; its great value is a number of money charts to help determine quick answers to the costs of home financing.

Single copies free from Chicago Title Insurance Company, Department R, 111 W. Washington Street, Chicago, Il 60602.

Tables for Graduated-Payment Mortgages, Including FHA Insurance Premium, 80 pages, September 1979.

Detailed costs of the new graduated-payment mortgages, using five different plans. Excellent help to understanding GPMs, how they work and what they cost.

$1.00 in check or money order (no cash) from Chicago Title Insurance Company, Department R, 111 W. Washington Street, Chicago, Il 60602.

A Home Buyers' Guide to Settlement Costs, 36 pages, May 1977.

Fairly simplified discussion of a complicated subject.

Free from Mortgage Bankers Association of America, 1125 15th Street, NW, Washington, DC 20005. Send stamped, self-addressed #10 envelope.

Real Estate Settlement Procedures Act, Special Information Booklet, HUD-433-NVACP (4), 30 pages, May 1979.

All about settlement costs. This is the booklet you must be given when you apply for a loan, but it's free to study ahead of that time.

Free from U.S. Department of Housing and Urban Development, Public Service Center, Room B258, 451 7th Street, SW, Washington, DC 20410.

Consumer Handbook to Credit Protection Laws, 46 pages, December 1978.

Not written especially for home buyers, but it will give you a good idea of the measurements applied to your application for mortgage money and a guide to your rights.

Free from Publications Service, Division of Administrative Services, Board of Governors, Federal Reserve System, Washington, DC 20551.

So You Want to Buy a Home, 17 pages, 1979.

Details the procedure of getting a mortgage loan from a savings and loan association.

Free from your local savings and loan association.

Moving Information

Summary of Information for Shippers of Household Goods, 28 pages, revised 1979, BOP 103.

Lost or Damaged Household Goods, 16 pages, 1979, Public Advisory #4.

1978 Household Goods Carriers' Performance Records, ICC News #208-79.

The Interstate Commerce Commission regulates interstate movers' costs and responsibilities. The first book above is a must if you're planning a move from one state to another.

All three are free from Interstate Commerce Commission, Public Information Office, Room 1211, 12th Street and Constitution Ave., NW, Washington, DC 20423.

After Your Move

Protecting Your Housing Investment, 27 pages, February 1979, HUD-346-PA(5).

Once you're in a home, good maintenance and care can protect your investment. This booklet is a good guide to what to do when about home care.

Free from the U.S. Department of Housing and Urban Development, 451 7th Street, SW, Room B-258, Washington DC 20410

NOTES

NOTES

NOTES

NOTES

NOTES

NOTES

NOTES